THE BLUE WALL

"Based on a secret Nazi U-Boat escape
at the end of WWII"

by

Ian Feldman

SSI Publishing, LLC

P.O. Box 815

Holly Springs, GA 30142

USA

Table of Contents

PART TWO: The Resolution

EPIGRAPH

HARZ MOUNTAINS, NAZI GERMANY – 1939

"We begin in a dark and forbidden place. An underground forge hidden deep in the Harz Mountains of Central Germany.

A massive sound is drowning out everything around us. It's the sound of hammering on metal, echoing throughout the caverns in this giant underground industrial grotto.

As we get closer to the production cavern of this forge, we can hear horribly emaciated prisoners in rag tag striped uniforms GROANING, as they POUR hot liquid metal into black ingot molds.

Then, even closer, we watch the metal as it cools, the liquid turns glassy, then hardens, as our image becomes completely visible. . . Gleaming GOLD BULLION BARS.

Then, even CLOSER: Indented into one's surface -- a NAZI SWASTIKA. And beside the Swastika, a line of numbers after a triangle-like emblem. . . The HEBREW Letter, shin 'W'."

The Harz Mountain Gold Bullion Forge

PROLOGUE

To our eye, nothing is visible yet.
We're in TOTAL BLACKNESS...

BLACKNESS so impermeable, it has no
boundaries. Then, the edges start to
push inward, to assault our view, from
all corners. White, invading Black.
then Red chasing White. Suddenly, we
pull back to a WIDER view to reveal the
dreaded -- NAZI SWASTIKA. It's stitched
to a flag, snapping from the upper
conning tower of a German U-Boat,
that's sliding upward out of the sea in
a stiff Ocean Gale.

As yet unnoticed, on this gloomy night,
this long dark form is surfacing out of
the depths of the Caribbean Sea into a
moonless overcast sky. A roaring spray
meets its bow, as the U-Boat begins
driving forward, onto the surface,
through black deep-ocean swells,
Southward.

Its TARGET, the North Coast of the
Dutch island of CURACAO; it's late May
1945 and the Second World War for
Germany is over.

We see the wave tossed hull of U-BOAT-
1055, Class VIIC/Modified, cutting
through the strong Caribbean Sea
currents. A Twenty-Five Knot tail-wind
is pushing its stern adding about Two
to Five Knots to the Boat's forward
speed. White caps FOAM all around the
bow, as they roll in and push outward.

Overhead, we observe two Anti-Aircraft
Gunners climbing into positions high on
the Conning Tower. Their conversations
are indistinct, as the U-Boat's
Commander exits out of the main Conning
Tower hatch below them and looks up at
the NAZI flag snapping in the wind.

KAPITAN WOLFGANG LÜTH turns and sights
his Binoculars along the misty
Coastline searching for his target, a
small inlet:

'ST. JORIS BAY'.

Closer, we view LÜTH's hand on the
forward railing, as we catch sight of
his distinct KRIEGSMARINE Ring; black,
red over gold.

He's got gentle eyes, features more of
an academic than a KRIEGSMARINE
Officer.

Rapidly, their dialogue begins in GERMAN, as the 1ST ANTI-AIRCRAFT crewman speaks.

"KAPITAN, we see it. A Light off our Port Bow at Ten Degrees. Red - Three Dashes."

Abruptly, the KAPITAN also sees the RED blinking light. Three dashes, then off; three dashes, then off. It keeps repeating. Finally, he sees the inlet. It's less than Two Kilometers Southeast of their position. It is narrow, with high canyon-like walls on either side.

The Crewman again quickly adds,

"KAPITAN, I see the channel to the Bay. It's very narrow.

And there's extreme white caps at the entrance. . . it could be too shallow."

KAPITAN LÜTH reacts with a commanding voice,

"It doesn't matter, Reinhardt. We're out of fuel from that Air Attack in the Mona Channel. We must refuel. Our Agents on Curacao will help us."

Suddenly out of nowhere the DISTINCT DEEP ROAR of an American Mariner Aircraft is heard. Reinhardt YELLS.

"KAPITAN, Mariner at forty-five degrees off the Starboard Bow. Do you want us to commence-fire?"

LÜTH again in a commanding voice,

"Hold Your Fire!"

Then he yells down to his First Mate in the Control Room below. . .

"Flank Speed - Heading - Ten Degrees, Southeast."

At that moment, the aircraft ROARS in close overhead, but doesn't fire or release its depth-charges.

But, after a wide turn, it comes back in for another pass, just as the U-Boat begins racing toward the narrow gap at ST. JORIS BAY.

Abruptly, the Mariner ROARS IN AGAIN, at less than two-hundred feet over-head.

It still doesn't fire or release bombs.

Without warning, both the Crewmen YELL, "KAPITAN, we're coming into the entrance too fast. All we see is white caps from up here. It can't be deeper than Fifteen Meters. . ."

The canyon walls of that channel will prevent us from maneuvering!"

The U-Boat is now less than Three-Hundred Meters to the entrance of ST. JORIS BAY, as the Mariner Aircraft breaks off and quickly disappears somewhere North.

It doesn't return.

The KAPITAN visually confirms, the Mariner is gone.

Then, seriously intense, he turns and shouts down the hatch to his First Mate — with obvious FRIGHT in his voice!

"All Ahead Stop!

Reduce Speed, Reverse All Engines!"

But it's too late. The STRONG WIND and the GUSHING SWELLS from the rear push the U-Boat to over Nine Knots. It moves over an outcropping near the surface of the narrow entrance, a RIPPING SOUND announces a MASSIVE GASH in the underbelly of the forward hull section.

Instantly, the Two-Thousand Ton U-Boat stops dead in the water. Engines go silent.

The KAPITAN's BODY SLAMS forward, then violently falls through the hatch into the control room.

Both Anti-Aircraft Gunners are HURLED
SCREAMING into the THRASHING WAVES and
hit the Canyon walls without a chance
for survival.

At once, the U-Boat seems to reverse
its direction for a moment. Then
without any warning, slides back. . .
downward into the black ocean depths,
vanishing from sight.

U-1055 at Sea, North of Curacao

PART ONE: The Deep Event

Chapter 1: ST. JORIS BAY - CURACAO

Bright sunlight.

The SOUND of WAVES CRASHING on the rocks.

We see JENNIFER VAN DER ROO, a young curvaceous girl - long blonde hair gusting in the wind - wearing a string bikini.

She stands seductively on a cliff overlooking the narrow canyon-like entrance to the Bay — intently, she's watching someone Kitesurfing.

From a more DISTANT VIEW - OCEAN SWELLS are being pushed in hard, Southward, by the winds of the Caribbean.

Then, in our view, a lone Kite-surfer appears. It's JON CHRISTIAN, Jennifer's boyfriend - blond hair, athletic build, an expert Kite-surfer. He's beginning a series of jumps and flips with his board as he navigates through the narrow channel.

Controlling the direction of his kite, he quickly enters the open Bay from a Caribbean Sea channel.

INSIDE THE BAY — we observe a group of three dogs, they're running down an isolated part of beach, playfully NIPPING AND BARKING at each other.

Jon then, turns his kite-board toward the beach where the dogs are running.

One of the dogs has something in his mouth. The dogs begin struggling and GROWLING to get hold of the object.

Jon releases his kite and runs ashore from his surfboard. He chases the dogs and grabs for the object from the lead DOG. Then SHOUTS at the GROWLING DOG in a Dutch accent.

"Caesar, drop it!"

We focus in CLOSE-UP: It's a HUMAN HAND.

Jon turns to see Jennifer running down from the cliff.

"Jennifer, get down here, now!"

Jennifer's voice has a distinct British accent.

"What is it, Jon?"

"It looks like there's been a Shark attack!"

Jon begins MUTTERING allowed to himself in Dutch, then. . .

"Uh, Damn . . . A man's HAND.

It's got some kind of Military Ring on its finger . . ."

Jennifer finally gets to Jon and COMMANDS the dogs.

"Back-Off!"

She focuses on what Jon is holding.

"OMIGOD, Jon. It's disgusting!"

Jennifer is PANTING from her run.

"You need to call your friend MIKE!

And get the Coast Guard over here, to search for the body."

Jennifer starts to dial her cell phone.

"Jennifer WAIT, hold off on that!

I've got to think this through. . .

There's something else going on here.

I want to talk to your Uncle about it, first."

"Why, Jon? There could be a man out there in distress."

Jennifer holds her cell, clearly ready to dial.

"If he's out there, He's dead by now.

Look at this, it's at least several

days old . . . Maybe more!"

Jon extends the hard grey leathery HAND out for Jennifer to see, as she turns away incensed.

"I can't look at that."

Jon grabs her arm and holds out the HAND, then points to the RING.

"Babe, you've got to help me. Use your cell camera. . .

At least get a shot of this for me."

Jennifer reluctantly sets her phone to camera mode, taking shots of the RING.

"There . . . I'm Done."

"I'm taking the DOGS with me, back to the VOLKS.

And you need to call Mike, anyhow, since this is where he and his crew patrols."

"Okay, Okay." Jon hesitates. . .

"Let me get my gear - I'll meet you at the car."

Jon YELLS at her, as she quickly moves away.

"Call your Uncle Dirk, Jennifer!"

"Here, then . . ." Jennifer tosses the cell phone back to Jon.

"Take it and call him yourself, Jon!"

Jennifer then grabs the collar of the lead dog as she walks away toward a little yellow Volkswagen, parked just off the beach, sitting beside an ancient dilapidated Dutch LANDHOUSE.

Jon fumbles with her cell, dialing a number, AS . . .

ST. JORIS - The Dilapidated LANDHOUSE

Chapter 2: CHRISTOFELBERG MOUNTAIN

We hear the sound of a CELL PHONE BUZZING. It's Not Being Answered.

The Cell is in a Rucksack mounted on UNCLE DIRK VAN DER ROO, a big six-foot-six man in his fifties, shaved head - strong chin, deep set eyes - ex-Dutch Special Forces. He's Jennifer's Uncle.

Several Other Military types with seventy pound Rucksacks on their backs are RUNNING HARD behind him up a cactus and brier filled Mountain side: Desert-Like Terrain, yet it's on the Island of Curacao.

VAN DER ROO is not even sweating as one of the Special Forces types WHEEZING, yells at him.

"Colonel, You're killing us with this. Twice a day in this terrain? In this Heat?

It's just like the Sinai in Ninety-One."

VAN DER ROO responds in a hard, but typical tone of voice, with a strong Dutch accent, that everyone expects from him.

"That was a righteous War, Robert!"

WE FLASHBACK TO: SINAI DESERT, NIGHT, ISRAELI BORDER, Near EILAT - 1991

VAN DER ROO and two Israeli Special Forces NCO's are perched on a Desert ridge observing.

Several Terrorist are unloading Russian Shoulder Fired Rockets from a small twin engine aircraft into a white van.

NIGHTSCOPE VIEW: VAN DER ROO sights in his M-14 Sniper Rifle at a terrorist in the plane's cockpit. Then views three other targets.

WIDER VIEW: The two Israelis move stealthily into the Terrorist Compound and get set for VAN DER ROO's action.

Suddenly - PHFT! -PHFT! -PHFT! -PHFT! - VAN DER ROO's sound suppressed M-14 takes out all four targets.

EXPLOSIONS AND SHOTS ROCK THE DESERT SILENCE as the Israelis destroy the van and plane, then the remaining Terrorist targets.

TERRORIST POV: But one is still hidden and alive. He comes up behind the lead Israeli, MOSHE.

Moshe is a physically solid, dark skinned, blue eyed KRAV MEGA expert.

Both Israelis have re-grouped on VAN DER ROO's side of the Compound, as the lone Terrorist tries to Garrote Moshe.

But Moshe senses he's there, as the Garrote pulls against his throat. Then that SOUND - PHFT! The Garrote releases. Moshe looks back into the Arabs eyes.

CLOSE-UP: One eye isn't there - only blood oozes out, as he falls away to the desert floor.

VAN DE ROO'S POV: Watches Moshe's face.

Moshe SHOUTS OUT in Hebrew, smiling at Dirk.

"I owe you one, my Crusader friend!"

DIRK VAN DER ROO smiles for the first time.

He watches the burning carnage in the distance, as his two Israeli Allies safely begin returning up the ridge.

CLOSE-UP: VAN DER ROO's Face - the view fades into a Gold Tooth in the upper jaw of his smile - then . . .
everything FADES TO BLACK, AS WE RETURN TO THE PRESENT. . .

Chapter 3: THE YELLOW VOLKWAGEN

PRESENT TIME - NEAR THE ANCIENT
LANDHOUSE - ST. JORIS BAY -

We hear The SOUND of Jon's kite
FLAPPING in the wind as he DRAGS his
Kitesurfing equipment up to the little
yellow four-door VOLKS. Then LOUDLY the
Kite DEFLATES as Jon begins storing it
in the trunk.

On the other side of the car, Jennifer
is almost nude, changing out of her
bikini into a sexy tube top and shorts.
. . while, the DOGS ARE BARKING in the
back seat.

Suddenly, Jennifer walks around the car
to where Jon is standing.

"Do you need any help?"

Jon, MUTTERING again in Dutch.

"I can't get him, Shit."

Jon then reacts in English to her
question.

"Just a towel, Babe, to cover this UP."

Jennifer grabs a towel from inside and
throws it at Jon.

"You'll have to wrap THAT, yourself.

I can't stand looking at IT . . . what a horrible thing."

But unexpectedly, she spies something where the Hand was ripped from the arm.

"What's that weird tattoo on the back of it?"

"It's the REASON, I wanted your Uncle to see this, first! He once told me a story about when his Dad was in WWII . . . When the War actually came here to Curacao. . .

He showed me a Ring just like this once, and said, if I ever found one like it on a DIVE, on a Beach or anywhere else on the island, I HAD to bring it to him before anyone else saw it."

"Understood, Okay. Then let's get it to him, Jon . . .

But before you get upset, we'll need gas, to make it all the way to OTROBANDA.

I didn't fill up the VOLKS. We're probably down to fumes."

Jon is intense and she can feel it, now.

At last, Jennifer hugs him. Then slowly kisses him seductively.

She turns and quickly slides into the VOLKS.

Jon finishes loading the trunk and secures his surfboard to the car's roof, then jumps in the VOLKS and extends over the backseat to hug the dogs before starting the engine.

In moments, they're off, driving on a dirt road leading away from the ancient LANDHOUSE.

The SOUND of the VOLKS MUFFLER and the DOGS BARKING at the wind, fills the air as they drive back to OTROBANDA.

Finally warming up, Jon puts his hand on Jennifer's thigh. She pulls closer, giving him a flirtatious kiss.

But then, Jennifer turns serious.

"What do you think he meant by that warning?"

Jon reluctant to open up.

"Well - You know his father Karl was part of the Dutch Command protecting the Isla Oil Refinery here on the Island. Karl also met one of the Nazi U-Boat crew they captured near Barbara Beach. . . There was an old photo he showed me . . . the Man had a Nazi tattoo and a ring. A Ring just like this one."

Jennifer jolts out . . .

"That's really weird finding this here at ST. JORIS Bay. We're miles from Barbara Beach. And besides, that's on the South side of the Island.

So, what do you think happened HERE?"

"I don't know, but let's get gassed up and ask your Uncle. Maybe we'll find out."

Chapter 4: THE GROCERY & GAS STATION

They arrive at a small isolated Grocery and Gas Station on the outskirts of a rough neighborhood. The place is three miles from the main highway to Willemstad and OTROBANDA. Jon pulls up to the single pump.

Some young local Punks are milling about. One of them sees the beautiful blond girl in the VOLKS.

"Go in and get me two POLARS, Babe!"

Jon's in deep thought about the RING and notices nothing.

"I'll fill 'er up! . . . Here, take a Ten for the Brews."

Jennifer gets out of the car and tries to avoid eye contact with any of the Punks. She quickly moves to the door of the Grocery. But, she's highly noticed as,

One of the Punks gets to the door opening first, speaking in the island slang accent - Papiamentu.

"Well hel'low, Miss beau'ti'ful lady."

Jennifer carefully enters the Grocery doorway, passing by a second cockier young Punk, speaking in slang to her.

"I think we are going to have a Par'tayh now, my Man."

Jennifer makes no comment as she rushes over to the Beer Cooler and grabs two Polar Beers, then walks quickly to the counter.

As she reaches the counter a Bearded Old Man greets her. He's respectful, but clearly intimidated by the punks.

"Dat'ill, be Four Guilders, my Lady."

The second Punk is behind her in an instant.

He places his hand on her back, then slides it down, as he purposely smells her neck.

Jennifer without reaction, pays the Bearded Old Man. Then snaps for the doorway,

As the second Punk speaks up. . .

"What a bod'day, my little lay'day."

The first Punk is crouching at the doorway. Jennifer looks at him, eye to evil eye. She passes him tense. He reaches out and strokes her leg as she passes, purposely.

Jennifer tries to distract him . . .

"Could you just get that door for me .
. . please."

Jon has just finished pumping the gas
and has paid at the pump, so now He's
walking toward Jennifer, as she emerges
from the store.

Suddenly, the older first Punk breaks
for the yellow VOLKSWAGEN and pulls
open Jennifer's door, trying to locate
her purse.

But all he finds is the towel wrapped
hand.

He grabs it and runs for the side of
the building next to another Punk with
crossed arms and a scowl on his face,
waiting.

The first Punk hands off the towel
wrapped object and stations himself in
front of the third Punk, guarding for
an expected attack.

Instead, Jon and Jennifer rush to the
car and get in.

Jon drives straight for the Building
and both Punks, then SQUEALS THE TIRES,
as he breaks the car in front of them.
Dust is everywhere.

The punks don't move. They stare
viciously at Jon. BARKING LOUDLY, the
dogs are silenced by Jon.

Jon gets out to confront the Punk holding the towel draped hand.

"You don't want that, Man! That's bad Juju! Real-Bad Juju!"

But this Punk is older and smarter - decides to open up the towel. He sees what's in it, as a vicious disapproving sneer comes over his face - he's vengeful.

His voice is a deep slang Papiamentu . . .

"You kill a Man, Boy. What you doin' wid' dis, Boy."

"Listen, Man!" Jon reacts hands in the air.

"We found that at ST. JORIS. We've got to get it to the local Police. You don't want any part of that. You know it, too!"

"Maybe so, Boy, but we take this RING."

At that moment, Jennifer jumps out of the car.

She sees the third older PUNK slide out his knife to cut off the ring finger, then She SCREAMS.

"No 'oooh . . . STOP!

That's my Dad! Don't touch him."

Jennifer starts crying.

"What you mean, Girl." Punk Three stops cutting the finger, as he looks at Jennifer.

"How you know that, Girl?"

Jennifer acts in pain, still crying and watching him.

"It's the RING! It's my Dad's Ring. It's the only way they can identify him!"

Punk Three looks closely at the Ring for several moments . . . Then back at Jennifer.

By now, Punk Two arrives to join the others. Together they look tuff. Clearly an experienced gang of thieves that control this isolated place.

Jon pulls Jennifer back behind him and moves towards Punk Three.

Suddenly, Jon opens his arms submissively.

"Listen, Man! How 'bout a trade."

"What? That Girl you have there!" Punk Three LAUGHS and the others LAUGH LOUDLY with him.

Jon's expression turns serious.

"How 'bout a twenty, Man!"

Punk Three snickers at Jon . . .

"You really want this or not, Boy?"

Jon reacts beaten . . .

"Okay then, I'll give you all we've got."

"How much, Boy?" Punk Three answers.

"A Hundred US Presidents." Jon plays it out.

Punk Three motions to Punk Two to get the money.

"Go get it then, Boy!"

Jon rushes to the VOLK's glove compartment and digs out all of his hidden US$ Twenties, then gets out and hands the money to Punk Two.

Jennifer walks carefully over to Punk Three and reluctantly holds out her hand to take the object, now rewrapped back in the towel.

Tears are still on her face.

"Would you please . . ."

She hesitates, as she watches him.

"Let me have it back now, Sir."

Punk Three smiles jestingly. . .

"You call me Sir. Ha, Girl, I'm CARLOS . . . Everyone 'round here knows that!"

Jennifer turns serious. . .

"Then Carlos, please let me have it back now."

That's better, Girl! You remember that too! -- You remember what I do for you, Girl."

Carlos looks her over meticulously, then pushes it into her breasts, as she takes it back quickly.

Jennifer rushes back beside Jon at the car, as he jumps into his seat while Jennifer slides in beside him from the opposite side.

Jon STOMPS the gas and turns the wheel away from the punks with TIRES SQUEALING and dust flying, as they quickly escape to OTROBANDA.

Just as they leave, Carlos steps behind the building and makes a cell phone call.

He's fishing for a bigger payout. . .

"I have something interesting for you. One of the young surfers driving through here from ST. JORIS BAY. Found a man's hand with a RING. . .

A RING like the one you told me to watch for. What's it worth to you, Friend?"

Clearly, the voice on the cell reacts intensely to Carlos statement. As Carlos comes back. . .

"Cool it Man . . . I can still get it. They just left here. . . they have to go through JAMAICA TOWN to get to the main road to OTROBANDA.

We'll get it there."

Again, the cell voice demands serious action as Carlos adds. . .

"I don't think we should make too much of this, or we'll get attention from outsiders down here.

We'll just delay them, while I get that RING for you. Leave it to me, they've got too much to lose to put up a serious fight."

Carlos flips his cell closed, then re-dials another number.

This time the Voice on the cell reacts subserviently to Carlos. . .

"It's me. Get some boys. There's a little yellow car with two pretty Dutch ones on their way. Block 'em and hold them for me. I'll be there quick."

Chapter 5: JAMAICA TOWN

Intense sunlight fills the windshield as Jon and Jennifer drive rapidly through open country toward JAMAICA TOWN. Only the SOUND of the MUFFLER fills the air as the dogs are quiet.

Jon is also silent and intense as he drives faster. Jennifer is still unnerved from the encounter, but serious.

"Now, maybe we should try Uncle VAN DER ROO! Again, Right Now, Jon?"

"You call him this time."

Jennifer speed dials his cell, but there's still no answer.

"Do you want me to leave a message?"

"No!" Jon freaks out.

"What's that up ahead Babe?"

Jon sees a local bus stopped in the middle of the road. Several people milling about. A woman waves them down.

"I don't think we should stop out here Jon. These people are making me very scared, especially after that gas station crowd."

Jon slows the car behind the bus for safety reasons. Jennifer turns to check behind them.

Without warning, a small white pick-up pulls in and SLAMS LOUDLY into their rear bumper.

"What the Hell?" Jon at once realizes they have no exit.

White shanty houses line both sides of the road. Locals stream down to see what's going on as the dogs begin BARKING LOUDLY out both rear windows. Jennifer's in tears. She SLAMS her fists on the dashboard.

CLOSE-UP: Jon opens the glove compartment, grabbing things, fast. MUMBLING in Dutch.

"Bastards! We're being set-up -- I know it!

They don't know me. They think I'm a dumb surfer, Hah! I'm a seasoned marine mechanic, Boys. And tricks, I've got!"

Jon finds a large brass gudgeon ring from his marine accessories box. He reaches down into the towel wrapping the Hand.

Once again the DOGS are BARKING INTENSELY.

In an instant, two very large black men jerk open Jennifer's door and grab her.

Jon tries to lunge across the seat at
them. But a big guy grabs his neck
through his driver's side window, then
pulls him back out of the car.

GRUNTS AND MUFFLED SCREAMS trail off,
as they all disappear into one of the
Shanty Houses.

A few minutes later Carlos arrives with
his posse and starts shouting orders.

"Get me that towel under the Girl's
seat!

And make sure that RING is still on the
hand!"

Punk Two makes a quick check in the
wrap to see if the ring is still there.
He starts to pass it over to Carlos and
hesitates.

"You want this phone too, Man?"

"Leave it!" Carlos looks back - then
struts to his car as he adds.

"Rough them up a little, but don't cut
them. And get their car off the road."

The DOGS CONTINUE BARKING as their
sound trails off in the background,
while Carlos drives off with the First
Punk. But it's the Second Punk that
enters the Shanty House.

It's a darkened Room. Very little
furniture. Several men standing around
Jon and Jennifer.

Ropes are tied around Jon and Jennifer's hands, pulling them taunt above their heads from cross beams in the ceiling.

GASPING to get her breath Jennifer tries to get free. Jon GRUNTS, as Ducktape is placed over his mouth.

The Second Punk enters the room. A cruel smile is on his face.

"Carlos said, Leave them to me."

The Punk motions the others to leave the room as he glares at the beautiful girl tied up in front of him.

Jon's eyes are piercing through the Punk, as he walks up behind Jennifer and pulls down her tube top in one quick motion. His hands move over both her breasts.

His face slides around her back as he LOUDLY SMELLS HER body up to her neck.

Jennifer WHIMPERS A SOFT CRY as his hands move from her breasts down her waist.

"Oh God, leave me alone you Bastard."

"At last, I get to touch your 'bod day', my little 'lay day'."

Without attention, Jon starts swinging back and forth until he can reach the Punk's location.

Then thrusts his feet at the Punk's back, knocking him down and away from Jennifer.

Finally, Jon gets his hands free and falls unbalanced to the floor as he rips off the duck-tape. But the Punk regains his position as he LOUDLY SLAMS Jon hard in the gut with two body punches.

Jennifer is SCREAMING LIKE A WILD WOMAN.

"Beat that Bastard, Jon. Use your Kung Fu!"

The Punk keeps PUNCHING and JABBING Jon backward. At last, Jon launches a series of KICKS and SHIN THRUSTS SMASHING the Punk to the floor. A final PUNCH in the jaw COLLAPSES the Punk down. He stops moving.

Jennifer's face is an expression of amazement as Jon looks up at her.

Jon's laughing. . .

"For the last time, Babe . . . It's Muay Thai!"

Jon smiles. He grabs Jennifer's rope and lowers her down, then releases her from the rope ties.

She immediately pulls up her tube top. Then runs to the Punk, giving him one last KICK, this time in his face.

She EXHALES A LOUD SCREAM OF SATISFACTION! Then looks back at Jon, as he adds . . .

"That's the spirit, Babe!"

Within moments, they're outside. Bright Sunlight hits their faces as they hear the DOGS BARKING and locate the VOLKS. It's just off the road behind a Shanty House in Jamaica Town. But the dogs are nowhere to be seen.

Jon is focused, as he gets into the VOLKS. But Jennifer runs toward a crowd of people swarming around an event. Dogs are BARKING AND GROWLING IN A FIGHT. Two Pit Bulls are pinning Jennifer's dogs down.

Jon SCREECHES the little yellow VOLKS into the melee as he commands.

"Get in the car, Jennifer! The dogs will follow you."

Jennifer opens the car's rear door. She then, JUMPS into the front seat YELLING at her lead dog.

"Get in here, Caesar!"

Caesar reacts leaping into the back seat as the other dogs follow, breaking off the fight. Then Jon YELLS, as he TRAMPS the Gas!

"Let's go . . . Hold on Babe!"

The car JERKS forward causing the rear door to SLAM SHUT. SQUEALING AWAY, they leave the crowd and JAMAICA TOWN behind.

Frantic, Jennifer FUMBLES AND SCRAMBLES around the car's interior.

"OMIGOD, I can't find my phone.

Those bastards took it."

"But they left the car, Babe . . .And they didn't kill the dogs. . .And we've got gas."

Jon utters a crazy laugh. . .

"And you weren't raped by that punk bastard!"

Suddenly, Jennifer LAUGHS DEMENTEDLY along with Jon, while searching the floorboard.

"Thank God! It's HERE. My phone.

At least we've got cell shots to show for this insanity.

Maybe Uncle VAN DER ROO can make something of this photo I took, if we ever get back to OTROBANDA."

Jon reacts intense. . .

"But first, we've got to drop off your dogs and store my Boards at the apartment.

Call your friend MARGRIT and ask her to
feed them. I have a feeling, it's gonna
be a LONG NIGHT, tonight."

Chapter 6: BANQUE DU CURAÇAO - PUNDA

BANQUE DU CURAÇAO - BOARDROOM

CLOSE-UP POV: A Large Video Monitor -
Four frames - Financials on three - An
individual on Camera - Top left view —
It's VORT BLAAU, Chairman of the Board
of Banque du Curacao.

Below BLAAU's screen image are the
words: *"SECURE TRANSMISSION"* -
Headquarters - Berne, Switzerland.

BLAAU's face is visually contorted. As
he speaks, TENSION is detectable in his
strongly accented Dutch/English
enunciation.

"You've put us at risk. You know that
now. Anyone outside of us, that touches
any part of this, must disappear!
Permanently! I'm placing that
responsibility on you, VANBOVEEN.

"Time is critical. There are others at
risk here too. No one can know of our
Reich Bank connection from the WAR.

Our sister firms in London and
Luxembourg and as well Banque du Rhone
in Geneva . . .

They will all want immediate closure.

I've been in Berne for over fifty years and this is the first time we've been seriously threatened!

Solve this quickly or the outcome could be very painful for your entire Group there in Curacao.

We cannot let any of this get out to the media. We must have a complete blackout, especially where the Israelis are concerned."

Suddenly BLAAU goes silent, his face shows intense concern. . . then, he reacts. . .

"I can't believe an actual Crew Ring has surfaced. This could mean the U-Boat is somewhere in the waters around Curacao, NOT in Venezuela as we had assumed from the German documents.

I'm now transmitting a list of the initials you should be looking for, inscribed on the inside of that Ring."

The Large Video Monitor begins blinking - The top right frame changes to: A List of Names with Initials beside each name -

Financials are only on the lower two frames - BLAAU is still on Camera - Top left view -

"These names listed here are the KRIEGSMARINERS that Admiral Donitz's officers identified in 1945 as Crewmembers on board U-1055. The Nazi's kept meticulous records. If any of these initials are present on your Crew Ring, then we have our TARGET.

When do you expect to have it?"

WIDE VIEW: Boardroom - cold and austere, but very modern in design.

HENRIK VANBOVEEN - Manager of the Curacao Division of the Banque du Curacao, glances anxiously back into the room.

Two silent security operatives sit like Human Clones in chairs behind him at the Boardroom table.

All are intensely watching the Large Video Monitor Screens. Henrik SPEAKS, his accent is Dutch, but his English is better than BLAAU's.

"The Courier should be here within the hour Chairman BLAAU. We'll contact you as soon as we have the Ring in our possession."

Instantly the two upper frames of the Large Video Monitor return to Financials. BLAAU is gone.

VANBOVEEN turns back toward his Security Operatives. . .

"Find that idiot Carlos and escort him in here yourselves! I don't want any mistakes this time. And stay in touch with me at all times out there."

Both operatives get up simultaneously and move out of the Boardroom.

A Secretary quickly enters after them, addressing Director VANBOVEEN as she comes to a halt at the doorway.

Chapter 7: THE KURA BAR - OTROBANDA

WE PAN INWARD FROM THE ENTRANCE: A
Darkly Lit Local Jazz Bar — Soft SOUNDS
of a Sax, a Piano and a Singer, with
people of all types socializing
quietly. Indistinguishable, we here
TALKING in the background and BAR
SOUNDS.

A CELL PHONE BUZZING - Several Military
types crowded in a large Bar Booth
together - REHASHING WAR STORIES as VAN
DER ROO picks up his cell. He
Interrupts his cohorts, as he speaks to
all.

"I've got to take this. Give me a
minute."

Stands up and quickly walks to the
nearest exit, as he answers his phone
with his typically hard response.

"VAN DER ROO Here!"

His ears are filled with Jennifer
GUSHING. It's a rehash of her recent
crisis and horror as UNCLE VAN DER ROO
has no visual reaction. He listens
intently, then. . .

"God, Jennifer! But you're SAFE, Honey!
Hold on a minute, Kiddo!"

He pauses a moment to orientate. . .

"Is Jon there with you? I know this sounds insensitive Jennifer, but let me talk to him first, before we ACT!"

He hears MUFFLED SHOUTING on the other end, as the Cell gets transferred from Jennifer to Jon.

"Where are you, Jon?"

Jon's answer comes quick, as Dirk reacts!

"Got it, Jon.

I'll meet you in fifteen at my place. And Jon, park in my personal parking spot in the covered garage. And use the back entrance, Son.

And Jon, NO side trips. Come straight here!"

VAN DER ROO pockets his phone and turns back inside. Immediately, he gains the attention of his Military Cohorts as he V's his fingers and looks - Eye to Eye - at them in action mode.

"PIETER, DERRICK, you're with me!"

Without looking back, he walks for the front door, as Two very powerful men quickly follow him outside the KURA BAR.

We have a DISTANT VIEW of the ENTIRE STREET: Without drawing attention, VAN DER ROO and his Two Commandos quickly move through some light tourist crowds up several side streets for Five blocks to his Townhouse. Their conditioning makes it a no sweat jaunt. Somehow they elude the eyes of British, American and South American Tourists walking nearby. He avoids their languages too, as he COMMANDS IN DUTCH to his cohorts.

"Set up a security perimeter around my garage and watch for Jon and my niece, Jennifer.

You know where the supplies are in my BMW?"

Both men acknowledge VAN DER ROO, as he continues.

"Get them safely into my back entrance. Then keep an eye out for any potential threats.

And Pieter, call me when Jon arrives."

Pieter - deep voice in Dutch.

"I'll keep you posted, Colonel!"

"And Pieter, tell him to leave the keys in his VOLKS. We may have to move it, to better cover."

"We'll take care of it, Sir."

At the Garage, VAN DER ROO splits off toward the inside of his Townhouse.

Pieter and Derrick take up positions out of sight, nearby.

JON'S VOLKS - DISTANT VIEW: A Sunset is glowing in the mountainous horizon of the far Western sky over Curacao. We can see the Willemstad highway as it passes near FORT NASSAU, at the High Bridge over the channel to St. Anna Bay.

The Sunset is almost blinding Jon, as he drives into the setting sunlight across the Queen Juliana Bridge.

"Pull your shade down for me, Babe. I can barely see, with the way that Sun is angled."

Jennifer briskly lowers her Sun shade, then adjusts his to keep him from being temporarily blinded by the glaring light.

Finally, the car quickly circles down the long curve into the Wharf area.

Concern is on Jon's face.

"He really sounded serious. I hope, I didn't screw things up?"

Jennifer looks surprised at his remark.

"How could you have screwed up? OMIGOD, Jon! You saved me from those Punks. They could have all ended up on me.

I could have been raped, if you hadn't gotten loose.

"No, not that Jennifer. It's what I did, before they dragged us out of the VOLKS that's got me worried.

"You're my Hero, Jon. It doesn't matter what you did!"

"Listen to me, Babe! Just before those guys got to us, I switched the RING for one of my brass gudgeon rings. A large one I use on old Hobbie-Cat rudders. They almost look identical at first. .
.

That Carlos punk bought it. That's how we got out of there so quick. He ran off without checking the Hand and RING."

Jon slows the VOLKS for their next turn.

"When he tried to cut the finger off at the Gas Station, he'd pulled it over the knuckle. That made it easy for me."

Jennifer looks back at him in anticipation.

"I hid the real RING in my accessories box. It's here in the glove compartment. . .

Reacting, she reaches into the glove compartment and opens the box.

She holds up the RING, then GASPS A NERVOUS LAUGH.

"JESUS, Jon . . . They're going to be pissed!"

"That's what I'm talking about, Jen. They could be on our tail, RIGHT NOW. And WE, wouldn't know it. I never saw Carlos' car . . . Just that white pick-up."

Jennifer jerks a glance behind them. They are out of the OTROBANDA curve and over the bridge. Several cars are breaking to avoid their rear bumper. Jon slows to get a rear view look himself. He turns back fast, then hits the gas and runs the RED LIGHT at the bottom of the hill. He REVS THE VOLKS ENGINE, then speeds over the next rise.

Out of sight from the RED LIGHT -- he yanks the car into an alleyway near her Uncle's Townhouse.

Chapter 8: CARLOS

BANQUE DU CURACAO - SECURITY COMPOUND

DISTANT VIEW: A car with two men inside
has been admitted into a fortress-like
outer walled area surrounding the
Banque Du Curacao.

The car is directed to an underground
parking garage. Hurriedly, it slides
into a Visitors space as both doors
open.

The men are greeted by a German
Security Operative.

The FIRST SECURITY OFFICER is tall with
a solid build, heavy German accent and
chiseled Germanic features as he
growls.

"Do you have it, Carlos?"

Carlos is just finishing his cell phone
conversation with the Second Punk. His
VOICE is MUFFLED, as they finish about
the Shanty House incident. Carlos' face
is contorted.

He stuffs his cell phone, as he and the
First Punk exit the car.

Carlos looks up into the hard face of the First Security Officer . . .

"I need to inform Mister VANBOVEEN, there's a serious problem."

The First Security Officer is clearly agitated – He SPITS back a response.

"And what might that be, Carlos?"

Carlos coughs . . .

"I need to tell him, myself."

The First Security Officer's look is hard and vicious.

"That's not possible! NOW, out with it or this meeting is terminated.

Carlos' obvious facial tension reveals – he's out of his element.

"Okay. . . Okay, Mon. Here's what's up. . .

We DO have this crazy Hand. . . But."

Carlos hesitates . . .

The First Security Officer GROWLS into his radio aggressively.

"You better get down here, Now!"

Then he focuses on Carlos face.

"Let's see it then, Carlos. And tell your friend to get back in the car.

Carlos quickly motions for the First Punk to get back in the car. Then Carlos slides out and moves to the car's trunk - cautiously.

"Just before we got here, I stopped to check that RING, myself. . .

Well, that cocky Kid, the young surfer we told you about. . ."

Carlos Pauses - then unlocks the trunk.

"Somehow, he switched the RING on us."

Again, the First Security Officer SNARLS into his radio.

"It's turned to 'SHIT' down here. Get here Now!"

Carlos hesitates as he adds. . .

"He's also slipped away with his Girl, from our Shanty House Holding area.

Carlos turns his head gradually behind him - now aware that the First Security Officer has a high caliber gun with a silencer, pointed directly at his head. He slows his opening of the trunk, as the Officer says -

"Just a precaution, Carlos."

Carlos is now shaking . . .

"Say, be careful there, Mon. There's NO harm here. Just that item you want to see. We need to work together on this."

Carlos CLEARS HIS THROAT as he notices another Higher Ranking Security Officer entering from a side door with two additional men.

"I wouldn't be here, if that wasn't true, Mon. You know that, Mon. We've got to find them 'wea'sels', before they contact the local MAN."

Carlos focuses on meticulously unwrapping the towel to expose the Hand. Only a brass Gudgeon ring sits on the index finger. But Tattooed on the back of the Hand is a Nazi emblem.

Suddenly, the cell phone of the Higher Ranked Security Officer STARTS CHIMING.

He then walks in behind the Car; surveys the situation to observe the exposed Hand, then turns the cell to SILENT MODE and speaks in Dutch.

"Sir, we have only the Hand. We're awaiting your orders."

VANBOVEEN'S OFFICE: VANBOVEEN responds on the MUTED CELL to his Higher Ranking Officer . . .

"The Boy and the Girl have been identified. We now know where they live and work. . . their car license as well.

It's now in your hands to clean this
whole thing up quickly, including this
mess in the basement. . . Make it sharp
and clean!

Good Night, Mister Anders."

BASEMENT GARAGE: Maliciously, Mr.
Anders, the High Ranking Security Guard
reacts, as he pockets his cell . . .

"Good Night, Sir."

Then looks at the First Security Guard
and casually nods his head . . .

PHFT! PHFT! PHFT! PHFT! Four silenced
high caliber shots go off, almost
simultaneously.

Carlos slumps to the ground and the
First Punk collapses onto the Car's
forward floorboard.

Silence returns, except for the typical
background SOUND of electrical and
hydraulic motors WHINING within the
building.

Mr. Anders carefully folds the towel
over the Hand and moves off to a nearby
Exit door, motioning for the First
Security Officer to join him.

As he leaves, the First Security
Officer looks back at the two remaining
men.

"Clean it up and dispose of it, and get back here straightaway. . . we'll need to move on this bigger problem before midnight tonight.

Chapter 9: VAN DER ROO'S TOWNHOUSE

TOWNHOUSE GARAGE: Finally, the Yellow VOLKS arrives into the Uncle's Parking slot, as Jon and Jennifer exit and are rushed up a back entrance by Pieter.

Jennifer's Uncle meets them at the rear door and ushers them into the Living room, where his live-in girl-friend from the Czech Republic - PETRA JANECZEK is introduced. For the moment, they just acknowledge each other - everyone is clearly tense.

UNCLE DIRK VAN DER ROO breaks the ice and motions Petra to bring in some drinks. . .

"Jon, this situation is very unstable. I don't know how much time we have. You both need to be secured in a SAFE HOUSE. But for now, let's keep it simple.

Show me the RING. . ."

Jon smartly removes it from his pocket and hands it over.

CLOSE-UP: Dirk pulls out a magnifying glass and begins checking its detail. His face is expressionless as he looks it over, focusing on the inside bevel.

He then moves to a nearby desk and pulls out a diary. For the first time he shows some facial change. He's intense, but satisfied with what he's seen.

"Here's what we've got."

Everyone's attention is glued to the Uncle, as Petra returns with some simple appetizers and drinks.

"Back in the war years, Jennifer's Great Uncle Karl had contacts in Nazi Germany as well as back here on the island.

They were both British and Nazi Agents. They called them DOUBLES. . .

Uncle Karl had a Diary. It told about a last ditch effort by Himmler's SS to plunder over one hundred tons of Nazi Gold Bullion Bars out of Germany to resurrect the Nazi Reich in South America."

Petra hands him a drink, as he continues.

"Their plan was to use a U-Boat to hold the Bullion as ballast. They needed a safe port in Venezuela - but the U-Boat never made it."

Uncle VAN DER ROO holds up the Diary. The room is silent.

"This Diary holds the name and initials of each man on U-1055. Those initials were etched in each man's KRIEGSMARINE RING. And until now, they've never been found."

He looks at Jon, then Jennifer. Her face is tense.

"So what does all this mean, Uncle?"

"It's both good and it's bad, Kiddo! With this RING showing up, we now have an idea that the U-Boat sank in Curacao waters - probably where you were sailing at ST. JORIS. . . maybe the bottom of the BLUE WALL?"

Jon grins at VAN DER ROO.

"I know that area very well, Dirk. That's a place no one would think of - it's an extremely dangerous area of currents and hazardous wind that no ship or certainly not a submarine could deal with easily and for sure without expert knowledge.

I have to fight it, when I Kitesurf beyond those cliffs at ST. JORIS. No one else will go out there.

And besides, my BOSS, JAN THIEL would never let us dive his Beebe in those waters. . . it's too deep."

Dirk adds his reaction to Jon's analysis - he's still intense. . .

"I think that's what actually killed them, Jon."

"So what's the bad part about this Uncle, besides those punks ripping my clothes off and chasing us?"

"The bad, Jennifer, is that over the Years, other extremely powerful people have had access to photographic copies of the actual documents written in this Diary.

They're also on the look-out for that U-Boat as well, and the massive amount of GOLD Bullion, at PRESENT worth BILLIONS of US Dollars, that was in it.

They too, have the initials of those crew members. . .

The problem we have HERE AND NOW. . . is we're unsure of who these people are, but I have a feeling we're soon going to find out!

Anyhow, that's why we've got to get you both to a SAFE location -- tonight!"

He abruptly turns to Petra.

"Let's pack up and get everyone out of here, NOW!"

BANQUE DU CURAÇAO - DIRECTORS OFFICE: We pan to a DESK.

CLOSE-UP: Computer Monitors on VANBOVEEN's desk - Passport Photos of Jon and Jennifer on screen - Jennifer is eighteen and Jon is twenty-two. VANBOVEEN is staring intently at the details of their work history. Jon works for a deep dive service owned by Jan Thiel. The Dutch couple's apartment location and nearby contacts are also on screen.

YANNA, a female Security Operative is standing behind Henrik VANBOVEEN watching his actions. YANNA is an Eastern European National in her twenties - muscular - very attractive. YANNA needs to know her assignment, but her facial reaction is muted and unemotional. Speaks English with a strong Russian accent.

"Nice looking couple, Henrik. Can I play, with them . . .

Or, do you want them eliminated, ONLY?"

VANBOVEEN is grim faced - stares into the monitor - then points to the screen.

"Just make sure it's clean with no leftovers to trace back here. That Boy you see here is from Holland, and he has no known relatives in Curacao.

However, the Girl is a bigger problem. Her Uncle lives here. And that man is ex-Dutch Special Forces.

I've got a dossier coming down from
Berne on him late tonight. He's
certainly got contacts here and may be
the next place they run to, if they're
not at their apartment.

Try both locations, but wait for Anders
team to be in place at the Uncle's
place before going up there, just in
case the Uncle has back-up."

YANNA reacts coldly. . .

"Should I just go there, first then?"

"No, YANNA. Get to their apartment and
find any useful intelligence. You know
the drill."

BACK AT DIRK'S TOWNHOUSE: Pieter sees
them first. Two cars, a Mercedes and a
White Utility Van pull off the street
near the Townhouse.

Several men scatter in various
directions toward the front and rear of
the building. The SUITS have radios and
begin COMMANDING, while two muscle men
with automatic weapons, move out.

Pieter motions to Derrick and then
contacts Dirk on his Radio-Cell. Dirk
reacts in surprise to the sudden
incoming call. . .

"I'm moving them, Pieter. . ."

Pieter lines up his silenced automatic weapon on various targets. He urgently commands back in Dutch to Dirk.

"Get them out now, Dirk! Four targets - two in front - two in rear. We'll cover the rear Garage Exit.

Your car is HOT and ready to roll."

WIDE VIEW OF THE GARAGE: Petra exits first, holding Jennifer's hand and pulling her into the waiting BMW. Jon, then Dirk rush out next. Petra takes the wheel, TIRES SQUEALING, drives to capture them both.

ON his Radio-Cell, in Dutch, Derrick speaks calmly to Pieter. . .

"I've got one almost at your six, Pieter. I'm taking him down, Quiet."

Just as the first big muscle man begins to move around the corner into the Garage entrance, Derrick catches him in a head lock and breaks his neck in one motion. He then pulls him in under some bushes out of sight.

Derrick repositions. He SIGHTS his silenced automatic on the SUIT at the Mercedes.

"He's down, Pieter. Do you want me to CLEAR that one at the Mercedes?"

"Hold off until Petra and Dirk clear the Garage, Derrick. . .

Then take out all Targets. I'm at your six in five counts. We'll take your car and back up Petra's exit."

PETRA GUNS THE BIG ENGINE just as Dirk and Jon enter. She aims for the entrance Derrick has cleared. Instinctively, she makes the turn for the opposite street avoiding the Mercedes.

WIDE VIEW: Derrick and Pieter open up as the BMW disappears, SCREECHING OFF into the night.

PHFT! PHFT! PHFT! PHFT! PHFT! PHFT! Several silenced high caliber shots go off forcing the remaining assailants back to their vehicles.

AT THE MERCEDES: The SUIT at the Mercedes is hit. The other muscle man runs back behind them. They're all pinned.

The other SUIT, Mr. Anders, calls VANBOVEEN on his cell, in Dutch. . .

"Mister VANBOVEEN, they're here, in force. We've lost one and Lugar is hit though his protective Kevlar.

Do you want us to pursue them?"

AT BANQUE DU CURACAO - DIRECTORS OFFICE: VANBOVEEN replies in English over his cell. His Face is fire red . .
.

"Shit! I should have expected this, once I knew they were Dutch Special Forces buddies.

Anders, we need some idea of where they are going. . . Follow, but don't confront them again, just yet. They obviously have armor piercing and more firepower than you, for NOW.

I'm going to try to have a Police road block set up, once you've got a direction and destination for me.

Now, go get those Bastards!"

AT JON AND JENNIFER'S APARTMENT: YANNA is in position inside. She's observing the lay out for computers and other information about the couple.

A lone man exits a nearby apartment and walks over to Jon's door. He knocks, then peeks into a window as YANNA passes by in the dark. Seeing her he yells.

"Hey, Hey . . . Who are you?

Where's Jon and Jennifer?

Alerted in kill mode, YANNA decides to confront him at the entrance doorway. She exits the door and stands casually in front of him.

"It's just me. . . I'm Jennifer's friend. Who are you?"

"I'm Jon's Technical Advisor, PROFESSOR HAGEN. Why were you in there with the lights off?"

"Just napping. Was getting something to drink. . . So, where do YOU, live, Professor?"

"Two doors down at One-Twenty-Two."

But the Professor gets more demanding.
. .

"Hey, where's the Dogs?"

That was YANNA's final cue. Instantly she thrusts a deadly kick directly to his neck . . . Breaking his windpipe in one movement, he gasps in absolute surprise, silently twisting in pain as he falls backward.

YANNA locks the apartment door, then grabs what's left of him and drags him back to One-Twenty-Two. The door is unlocked as she pulls him inside, just as the lights of an arriving car, almost catch her closing his door.

INSIDE DIRK'S BMW - RACING OUT OF OTROBANDA: Dirk commands aggressively as they leave.

"Petra, double back to Fort Nassau and take us to Nick's Salvage Yard. I'll call him and set up an Exit and a Dive Boat."

Dirk is in the front seat making his call on a cell. Jon and Jennifer's eyes are wide and tense in the rear. Petra is in her element driving with abandon, as they race down to enter the FORT NASSAU ROAD.

Petra escapes any sign of her pursuers on the Main Highway by turning into a hidden exit. LOUD SWERVING begins as they rush downhill on a narrow ROAD, wildly jerking around tenuous curves, hairpin turns and switchbacks as they make their way to the bottom of a valley on an inner Bay of the Island, below FORT NASSAU.

At last, shutting off her lights, Petra glides silently into an alley beside some dilapidated docks across the channel from the Isla Oil Refinery.

A Man stands in their exit, a warehouse doorway; then motions them to follow him into NICK'S Salvage Dockyard. . .

They quickly disappear inside, as massive metal doors GRIND CLOSED behind them.

Chapter 10: NICK'S SALVAGE YARD

A WAREHOUSE BELOW FORT NASSAU: Several people are milling about, INDISTINCTLY TALKING near an inside dry dock holding an advanced technology styled Yacht about one hundred meters in length.

NICK CHRISTIAAN, a hard salt-worn Fifty-something Naval Expert and Wealthy Entrepreneur, comes over to greet everyone.

He starts with Dirk, as they all unload out of the BMW. Nick's English has a distinct Dutch accent.

"Ah, my old Colonel! It's great to see you Dirk."

"And you, my old friend. It seems like the old days in the Gulf with the Yankees, again. Except this time, it's Rogue Europeans or Russians, not Iraqis."

"And who do you think it is, Dirk?"

"Really don't know yet, Nick, but I suspect they're highly connected and certainly have plenty of Tech and Muscle for this little Island.

But enough of that, Nick. We've got to secure these TWO!"

Dirk looks over at Jon and Jennifer, as he stresses the desperate situation. . .

"Most 'Riki 'Tik' –

Then, WE'LL go Salvage something in Deep Water.

WHERE, can we talk, Nick?"

"My office."

Nick turns to face Petra - then points to a doorway.

"And Petra, take everyone to that Customer Lounge over there and get yourselves some coffee and pastries. We'll be back shortly."

Jon quickly jumps in . . .

"Nick, mind if I join you two?"

"Sure Kid! Come on up . . ."

Nick Looks at Dirk VAN DER ROO. . .

"Can this Kid hold his whiskey?"

"Probably better than me, Captain!"

WIDE VIEW: Nick leads the way up a side staircase to an office overlooking the entire Dry-dock expanse.

Dirk and Jon follow looking back at the beautiful lines on the streamlined Yacht as Dirk adds . . .

"That's one beautiful piece of equipment, Nick. Who owns it?"

Nick unlocks the door, then flips on the office lights.

"Funny you asked, Dirk. A Saudi Prince! Bought it at the Dubai Yacht Show. I've had it for three months now, and they've yet to pay me a Florin, in upgrades.

Guess I may have to Repo the damn thing, just to make up for my expenses."

Nick moves in behind his desk and pours three Whiskies at his back-bar.

Dirk moves to a chair and addresses Nick, as Jon pulls one up from nearby.

"Hold that thought, Nick.

You know the U-1055 Story, don't you?"

Nick hands a full Whisky glass over to Dirk as Jon jumps up to help, grabbing another from his left hand. Nick picks up his own then falls back into his Main Captain's chair. As he responds 'matter-of-fact' to Dirk.

"You mean the Legend. I've lost track of that one, Dirk."

"Well, move it to front and center, Captain. We've got solid evidence it's actually in Curacao waters, NOT Venezuela."

"Damn, no wonder you've got all Hell coming down your back, Dirk.

That Legend, is scary stuff. Even the Israeli Mossad and their Shin Bet Assassin Squads are involved in it, these days!

There's some pretty nasty people that wish that Legend would go away. For starters our own local Bankers and even the Central Bank might be part of your problem.

They've always tried to cover up where they got their assets. . .

Some think it was that Nazi Holocaust Gold that launched our own Swiss powerhouse bankers here in Curacao after the real War."

"Well here's the way I see it, Nick.

Dirk at last, pulls the RING from his pocket, then hands it to Nick.

"Jon here and Jennifer were almost killed today after they discovered a rotted Hand at ST. JORIS with this UNDERSEEBOOT RING on its index finger. . .

I'm now convinced that U-1055, actually sank here, not in waters near Venezuela, as the so called Legend has it."

Jon jumps in adding to Nick.

"And most probably, off the deep BLUE WALL at the entrance to ST. JORIS Bay."

Dirk chimes in to stress their point.

"What would you say the maximum depth of that water out there is, Nick?"

"At least Two-Thousand Meters, maybe Three, right off the cliffs there to the dead bottom. There's no known shelf. It's a solid drop off right from the entrance to the Bay.

That's why they call it, The BLUE WALL."

Nick fiddles with the RING - stares at the initials in the bevel.

"You've verified that this man was on board?"

Dirk pulls out the Diary from inside his shirt, as Nick watches intently.

"It's all right here. In Dad's girlfriends' War Diary. You know that's a fact. I've shown it to you before -- She was a 'Double' and he was her contact inside Germany.

The KRIEGSMARINE and what was left of the German ABWEHR helped Himmler's people plan and remove all that Gold Bullion in early 1945.

Even the head of the Navy, Admiral Donitz was in on it. He let them change the official logs on U-1055's fate, then allowed them to modify and load it at Kiel.

In fact, at the END, Donitz was chosen and sworn in as the New Fuhrer, by Hitler himself. It was one of Hitler's last calls, when he swallowed his own cyanide capsule and took a bullet to the head. . .

Donitz was forced to 'Unconditionally Surrender' Nazi Germany alone to the Allies. By then, that U-Boat was on its way to Venezuela."

Jon again jumps in for emphasis. . .

"And they made sure every Crewman on board that U-Boat wore an identified KRIEGSMARINE RING with their initials. Dirk proved this RING is authentic!

It's a Crewman's RING from U-1055."

Nick breathes deep, as he slowly buys into the story . . .

"Okay, then, Dirk. Let's assume it's there. We're talking a lot of equipment and that's going to draw a lot of attention.

At least the Coast Guard and most likely these idiots you've got chasing you."

Dirk smiles at Jon, then Nick. . .

"You're right, Nick. But that's why I'm here. You're the expert in that. I'm the expert in muscle and tactics. And it looks to me like you've already got one piece for us; right here in dry-dock. The only other things we need are dive gear, master divers and a salvage boat.

And you've got all that too."

Nick is gasping for effect . . .

"You're crazy, Colonel. We'll need a deep ocean Bathysphere to get down there. And then what?"

Again, Jon slides in . . .

"If that's what it takes, Nick, then me and the Professor can take one of Jan Thiel's BEEBES . . . And dive it down there too".

Dirk grins back at Nick, as he finishes his drink and heads for the door.

"So, Nick, it's in your expert hands now. I've got to get these Two kids to a SAFE-HOUSE and you've got planning to do!

As Dirk heads down the stairs with Jon, they can hear Nick talking incessantly to himself - MUMBLING in Dutch -

"We'll need TRIMIX, Rebreathers, maybe HELIOX, Back-up ADS Divers suits, maybe even WASP salvage suits, maybe a Divers Bell?"

Chapter 11: KIEL - APRIL 28, 1945

BACK IN TIME - THE WHARF AT KIEL, GERMANY NEAR THE BALTIC SEA: Heavy rain showers are falling. In the distance, German ARTILLERY FIRE CAN BE HEARD. It lights up the sky periodically.

Suddenly a Secret Convoy of several camouflaged Nazi Military Vehicles LOUDLY GRIND UP to a Base 'Check Point'.

A High Ranking Nazi SS Officer halts their movement. He immediately begins inspecting the rear of each Truck.

Inside the rear of the first Truck, the Nazi SS Officer turns on a flashlight and opens a heavy wooden crate. Inside, he inspects several metal ingot bars, then scrapes them.

CLOSE-UP: They're Gold Bullion Bars with Nazi Emblems. He uses a testing device, then re-covers the crate. As he opens the rear curtain to exit, another Officer joins him. Together, they move to the next Truck, then motion the release of the first vehicle.

HEAVY RAIN, lightning and THUNDER continue. The lower ranking Officer gets in the lead vehicle.

He salutes the High Ranking Officer and gives the ALL CLEAR arm motion.

The Convoy vehicles GROWL loudly, as they START up and quickly move out into the dark night.

The High Ranking Nazi SS Officer and two of his Soldiers, march sharply toward a dimly lit small office near the dock.

The soldiers stand guard outside, as the officer enters. Inside, he opens a diary, then makes some notes, and begins DIALING on a rotary dial military phone. He makes two calls.

He dials, then waits for contact as he speaks in German over a secure military telephone line.

"Admiral, the Inventory has cleared Kiel and is on its way to the Fjord."

The Admiral on the other end acknowledges his transmission and hangs up.

The Nazi Officer then DIALS a second line and waits for the contact, then commands in German.

"This is SS-Gruppenfuhrer FEISLER!

Get me KIEL -- Number, 734, at once!"

An operator acknowledges in German, then switches the call to a private outside phone line.

The SS Officer changes to English with a broken Dutch accent.

"My friend, the belly of the whale will soon be filled with 'One-Hundred Herring'."

A female voice on the other end responds back with a British accent.

"We'll send for you in two days, Karl. Out!"

A SECRET U-BOAT BUNKER - FLENSBURG FJORD: Rain and THUNDER continue as the convoy from Kiel finally arrives and files quietly into a reinforced concrete bunker. Inside, U-1055 and its crew, along with the convoy drivers, unload the trucks into the rear deck hatches and a watertight doorway near the stern of the U-Boat.

The U-Boat KAPITAN and two officers are SHOUTING ORDERS to the drivers and the crew from the U-Boat's Conning Tower. At the open end of the U-Boat Pen, the SOUND OF HEAVY RAIN AND THUNDER ECHOS back into the cavernous chamber. The KAPITAN angrily yells orders at his men, in German.

"Faster, Faster! We've got to make the tide! Begin sealing the hatches and make ready for launch.

Prepare the SCHNORKEL!"

A large pipe-like object, with rubberized material insulating the upper portion of the metal pipe, taller than the periscope, is secured near the Conning Tower. Crewmen begin CLOSING HATCHES on the stern. The final crate is loaded through the watertight door and the door is SLAMMED SEALED.

The U-Boat's MOTORS COME TO LIFE and crew members begin releasing ropes to the dock hands, then climbing back into the Conning tower.

Only the KAPITAN and two anti-aircraft gunners are outside on the Conning Tower.

Abruptly, The U-Boat LURCHES FORWARD sliding silently into the Flensburg Fjord in the dark of night and toward the black Baltic Sea.

Unnoticed, U-1055 heads swiftly out of the FJORD.

Without warning, a LOUD EXPLOSION bulges flames into the night air to their rear, engulfing the entire U-Boat PEN.

The KAPITAN watches with his
binoculars, then nods to his two Anti-
Aircraft Gunners in rain gear, as they
all make a last scan of the sea and the
storm filled skies around U-1055.

The KAPITAN glances back, as the
FIREBALL finally disappears. He then
motions them to drop into the hatches
and dive the U-Boat beneath the waves
of the Baltic.

Only the SCHNORKEL, feeding air to the
DIESEL ENGINES, can be seen creating a
small wave ripple on the ocean's
surface as the U-Boat sails smoothly
into the mist.

Chapter 12: SAFE HOUSE - SANTA BARBARA

PRESENT TIME - KORAAL SANTA BARBARA:
It's late and dark as Dirk and Petra unload several bags of weapons and equipment into the downstairs living room of an old Dutch LANDHOUSE named KORAAL, overlooking Barbara Bay. It's a 40's era styled living room. A Spanish design with few windows and heavy wood book shelves.

Jennifer and Jon enter the room, then move up the stairs to the bedrooms.

Jennifer is stressed as she speaks. . .

"I've got to get that ampicillin, if we're going to be here long, Jon. I've still got three days left on my prescription."

"I Know, I Know, Babe! We'll get it."

And I need some other things too, Jon; my Laptop, so I can at least find out who these Bastards are that are stalking us. You're better at convincing UNCLE VAN DER ROO to let us go back there, then I am."

"I'll talk to him, Jennifer. Maybe Petra and I can make a run over there.

I'm sure those Bastards have already been there, so it should be clear by now."

Petra and Dirk enter the bedroom as they're talking, then adds his thoughts.

"It's not a good idea, Jon, but it sounds like you and Petra need to make a quick visit back to your place. My advice is Petra checks out the place first, then get what you need and get back here, 'Riki' Tik'!

Go, while it's still dark."

Petra looks at Jon, then to Dirk.

"I'm ready, Dirk.

Let's go, Jon!"

Petra and Jon head downstairs.

Jennifer starts fooling with her cell camera, to check out the photos she took from the beach as her Uncle comments. . .

"Mind if I see that photo of the Hand, Jennifer? It's got me a little baffled."

"What do you mean, Uncle?"

Jennifer hands him the Camera. . .

CLOSE-UP: He concentrates on the photo screen, as he zooms in and scans the length of the Arm and the Hand's leathery surface.

"The condition! I'm trying to understand the deterioration after so many years. Almost seventy, to be exact. There's only one thing that makes sense."

"What's that, Uncle?"

"The Blue Wall, Jennifer. Its depth is unknown. It's never been dived. And due to the severe wind and wave turbulence out there, versus so many wonderful dive spots on the South side of Curacao, no one has ever cared about diving it."

"It's for Kitesurfing, Uncle, and just a private romantic place for couples."

Dirk goes silent, as he watches her.

"Yeah, I guess you're right, Jennifer. . . Speaking of romance though, I wish you two would get married rather than just live together. . . your Dad would have wanted that, you know."

"He's good for me, Uncle. . . we love each other, and that's all that counts right now. If we were married, he wants kids, and we can barely afford the dogs for now."

"I'm not letting up on this, Kiddo."

Jennifer quickly changes the subject . . .

"So how deep is it? Where Jon and I Kitesurf, I mean."

"The Wall, I would guess at least One to Two-Thousand Meters, right at the mouth of the ST. JORIS Canyon."

"You're kidding! I've never worried about it, 'til now! Jon and I surf that area all the time and I've walked the edge of those cliffs above it, many afternoons. The water's always a rich deep blue color out there, but I've never realized how dangerously extreme it is, so close to shore."

"Oh yes, Kiddo. As a matter of fact, when you were scuba diving with us on the South Side near Barbara Beach, the water temps down to thirty meters, were almost 80 degrees. . .

At the Blue Wall, the first cold water thermocline starts at three hundred meters, dropping the temp to below 40 degrees.

Below One-Thousand Meters the temp can drop to almost sub-freezing. You can't Dive it without self-contained Atmospheric Suits or a Deep Ocean Bathysphere.

"OMIGOD, Uncle, that's crazy cold!"

"That's my point, Jennifer! Even here, in the Southern Caribbean Sea, below One-Thousand Meters, something sealed in a container such as that U-Boat, becomes like a canned sardine: preserved in its original condition until it's opened."

"So, something opened that U-Boat?"

"That's right, Jennifer. Either a sub-surface quake, a rough storm, or just a wall collapse onto the outer shell of the U-Boat, broke it apart. That's what probably released a body, or parts of a body —

That HAND."

Dirk pauses, did he hear a sound outside?

"That's why we've got to get Nick's Deep Diving Salvage team out there, Quick!

If the ship's damaged enough, it could deteriorate further and sink into impossible depths for recovery. . . at least using the recovery technology we have today.

Time is critical."

Within less than an hour Petra and Jon return to the SAFE HOUSE. They enter through the front door with a bag, Jens Laptop and her Antibiotic.

Waiting in the living room, UNCLE VAN
DER ROO and Jennifer sit talking on the
couch with drinks in hand.

Dirk comments first. . .

"Did you get everything you needed,
Jon?"

"We Got it, including the Laptop,
Dirk."

"That's great, Jon. I want you to do
some research for me, on that thing."

"It's not mine, Dirk. It's Jennifer's.
Your niece is the computer Guru! Not
Me. I'm the Sailor, Mechanic and a
Beebe Mate. She's the brains of our
outfit."

Dirk's face is filled with astonishment
as he looks at Jennifer.

"Damn, Kiddo . . . You're full of
surprises for your Old Uncle.

"Here's your assignment, then. I'm dead
certain our adversaries are somehow
connected with the Nazi history behind
this Gold Bullion. You need to find out
who they are? And what we're up
against?"

"No problem, Uncle. Have you got WiFi
or a Cable hook-up here in the House?"

Her Uncle is dumbfounded - he then
looks to Petra for help.

"Tell her, Petra."

"It's in the upstairs Office next to the Master Bedroom. It should be operational, but we must find it."

"Then get on it, Kiddos. I've got some outside perimeter work to do. . . Petra, show them where to set-up."

Dirk heads out to the rear of the Safe House Grounds. Everyone else moves to the upstairs Office and Master Suite.

But unknown to Petra and Jon, they've picked up a straggler on their drive back.

YANNA has followed them from the apartment and parked her car off the dirt road to the LANDHOUSE.

She's up a hill and positioned herself in some bushes overlooking the SAFE HOUSE. Observing them through Night Vision Binoculars from her vantage point and speaking softly, she calls Henrik on her cell.

"I'm now re-positioned near their SAFE HOUSE at Santa Barbara."

BANQUE DU CURACAO - SECURITY OFFICES: VANBOVEEN is calmly aggressive, as he responds to her.

"Just stay in contact with them, observe only!

Take no action, unless they discover you! We need to find out who else they have employed to help them, before we close in.

And tap those cell transmissions with that new gear I gave you!"

YANNA acknowledges and signs off.

VANBOVEEN motions for his secretary through the bulletproof glass wall of his Security Office. He's on a private cell call. She enters, as he commands her in Dutch.

"Get me the Commandant of the Dutch Coast Guard, Admiral GRAF at his WESTPUNT home. Excuse the late hour, but advise him he owes me a serious favor. Then give me the call on my private line."

Henrik turns away from her as she quickly leaves the soundproof room. But now he's fuming, as he speaks English into his cell to Mr. Anders.

"We know where they are, now! Get back here at once, and let's set up a plan to get control of this situation, once and for all.

NO loose ends this time, Anders!"

Hendrik puts Anders on SPEAKER.

"Agreed, Mr. VANBOVEEN! They've escaped this time and those Dutch Commandos disappeared as well. But we'll have twice the attack firepower in place next time. We're on our way back in."

As he ends Anders call, Henrik immediately starts TALKING IN DUTCH INDISTINCTLY to two new on-screen images, while four other monitors feed him financial information. The two incoming images are labeled at the bottom of each screen: GENEVA and BERNE.

PART TWO: The Resolution

Chapter 13: NICK'S ADVANCED TECH YACHT

ISLA REFINERY BAY — LATE NIGHT: It's three AM. An enormous steel door GRINDS OPEN at Nick's salvage yard. The WHINE of HIGH PITCH TURBO ENGINES can barely be heard, as a sleek high technology Yacht glides out of Nick's facility at the protected base of Fort Nassau.

Several crewmembers stand watch on deck for any potential threats, while checking clearance and depth. The massive door GRINDS CLOSED.

The Yacht moves silently into the Isla Refinery Bay. Inside at the ships helm, Nick watches his team take her out.

On the YACHT'S BRIDGE, several crewmembers are watching various high tech monitors while working keyboards and joysticks. Nick himself sits at a high tech command center moving a joystick to control direction and thrust of the Yacht, as he contacts Dirk though his headset cell phone.

Nick has a wide grin on his face - almost a smirk, as he speaks to Dirk on his headset.

"Okay Colonel, we're in the water and moving to the rendezvous point. Oh, and our transport's that new High Tech Saudi you took a fancy for. No sign of your problems, here."

SAFE HOUSE - KORAAL SANTA BARBARA: Dirk responds quietly into his cell.

"That's great, my old friend. But let's keep this short, Nick. I think we may have a visitor and I'm going to need back-up."

THE YACHT'S BRIDGE: Nick quickly reacts.

"Clear, Colonel! Just, one thing to add though. The Coast Guard might be a problem. We picked them up on our scanner twenty minutes ago and they are on the hunt for ships that are in a ten mile range of ST. JORIS.

Someone got to the local Commandant."

SAFE HOUSE - KORAAL SANTA BARBARA: Dirk responds back quietly.

"I'll talk to Jon about using ZAAN Thiel's Bathysphere. Maybe you should set sail and meet us the Southern Dive Operations Center down at Newport Bay.

If we can divert the Coast Guard's attention long enough, we could run that Bathysphere along the Blue Wall under their ship's surveillance. . .

Safe travels, Nick."

THE YACHT'S BRIDGE: Nick begins to move the Advanced Tech Yacht into the main channel through Willemstad, silently passing city lights and the old buildings of the Caribbean's answer to Amsterdam.

The Yacht moves quickly, but creates hardly any wake as it maneuvers past several conventional Yachts and Oil Tankers docked alongside the main channel of St. Anna Bay.

"Got that Colonel. Great distraction, I'll be in contact with ZAAN on that one. He should be there by 0700.

Keep safe, Colonel! Out."

SAFE HOUSE - KORAAL SANTA BARBARA: Dirk CLICKS his cell twice, then silently signs off.

THE YACHT'S BRIDGE: Nick turns to his first mate and commands him to open the Queen Emma pontoon bridge with the ships remote control. He then makes another cell call to ZAAN THIEL at the Bathysphere Operations Center at Newport.

Nick slows the Yacht, as they wait for the Queen Emma to open. Then advancing slowly to get through the passage, he guides the Yacht quickly out into open water. In moments, the powerful twin turbine ENGINE SOUNDS ARE HEARD as it REVS UP and turns Eastward, disappearing quickly into the black night waters off Curacao in the Southern Caribbean Sea.

SAFE HOUSE - KORAAL SANTA BARBARA:
Inside the Master Suite, the only light in the room is the Laptop screen and a small tensor lamp on a desk that Jennifer's working at. Jon is asleep in the king-sized bed.

But, Jennifer is adrenaline charged, as she adeptly flips through Google Screens and Other Search Engines, while quickly typing command codes and gathering tons of information on her Uncle's assignment.

The screen flashes with information on the Swiss Banks involvement -- U-1055, The Lost Nazi U-Boat, Banque Du Curacao, Banque Du Rhone, The Israelis, The Mossad, and finding Himmler's Stolen Holocaust Gold.

Suddenly, Jon sees her light is still on and groggily calls to her. . .

"What Are you doing, Babe. Come to Bed.

We only have a few hours before this situation gets really crazy!"

Jennifer is supercharged and can't sleep.

"I've found them, Jon. I've found all of it. All of their nasty ugly secrets and why they've kept this concealed for so long. It's the Banks. They are the ones chasing us. They are the ones that need to hide this Nazi Gold Story. It's probably Holocaust Gold or Looted Gold from Sovereign Nations that the Nazi's murdered thousands of innocents for.

If it ever gets out to the News Media, The World Press, or The Israelis, then EVERYONE will want a piece of it.

We'll never get control of that Gold, Jon, unless we sneak it out of that U-Boat before anyone knows it's gone!

Jon drags himself over to her monitor screen. He watches as a parade of images flash by, then touches Jennifer's neck softly. She FLICKS her hand to shake him off. It causes him to frown and move away.

"GOD, Babe, you've really got into this."

"This is serious Shit, Jon. What are we going to do? How can we justify taking this Gold, without considering the repercussions?

Is this Really, what we want!

I've got to talk to UNCLE VAN DER ROO, before we go any further with this. I've got to show him what I've found."

SAFE HOUSE — LIVING ROOM: Petra enters the Living Room after checking the elevator's operation, then turns on the front outside lights.

Suddenly, she notices some movement on the hill above the top of the driveway. As she enters the Garage, she quickly she turns out the front road lights, and releases WOLF, her Alsatian Guard Dog, from his pen to check it out. Wolf is silent, but quick. He returns back in a few moments.

She immediately calls Dirk on her radio cell.

"Something's not right up here, Dirk. I just let WOLF run the perimeter and he's back too quick. - I think we have company."

SAFE HOUSE — OUTSIDE: Dirk acknowledges her call over his cell.

"Make sure that elevator is operational. Get Jon and Jennifer, NOW! I'm coming to you.

SAFE HOUSE — INSIDE: Petra motions Wolf to follow her, as she heads back inside. Petra arrives at the staircase below Jon and Jennifer's Bedroom. Wolf follows her as she rapidly moves up the hallway. Petra checks the elevator again, then responds to Dirk.

"I just checked it. It's Ready!"

"Petra, Take them down to the lower escape tunnel. If I'm not there in five minutes, move out to the Jet-boat dock and go directly to NEWPORT, and have Jon meet with his boss on our need for the Beebe.

SAFE HOUSE — OUTSIDE PERIMETER: Dirk uses a pair of night-vision binoculars and scans the horizon toward the front of the property. Someone is there watching the house.

Dirk is still undetected.

Suddenly several more objects move across his night-vision horizon. They quickly take up positions around the property.

The first person he saw, is directing them with hand movements.

Dirk remains silent.

He quickly mounts a combination sound & blast suppressor to his modified M-14 night-vision Sniper Rifle, aligning his Night-vision scope to locate the closest target. He's at twenty yards. It's now or never.

PHFT! PHFT!

Two silenced high caliber shots go off.

The man is down, but his cohorts are now firing. They are not sure where it came from, but they too have silencers and mounted night-vision viewers on their faces.

They stop moving and go defensive, searching for the shooter.

SAFE HOUSE – MOVING AWAY: Dirk begins moving from the Safe House into the bush. He's looking for a clear open space so he can take them out. They see him moving, but can't follow where he went.

He crosses an open ravine and takes up position at a rock wall with good fields of fire into the open ravine. He sits tight.

Are they coming? Suddenly he sees the first one. He's got Night-vision mounted on his eyes, but no scope. Dirk aims his Night-vision Sniper Rifle.

He waits. The second one enters the ravine. They are both in his kill zone.

PHFT! PHFT! They are both down, but the second one is still moving.

PHFT! PHFT! Nothing else moves in. Dirk doubles back to the Bay side of the Safe House.

Flashes from the hillside. RATTATTATTAT! RATTATTAT! The bushes beside Dirk EXPLODE. They've ranged his location.

Dirk hits the ground and low crawls like a mad Cayman Crock to a rock outcropping. He SIGHTS in their positions from where the Flashes came from. He sees them. Several more have entered the kill zone.

PHFT! PHFT! PHFT! Again, Dirk opens up with three lethal sniper hits. They stop moving forward and begin backing off over the hill to the entrance of the drive.

SAFE HOUSE — BAYSIDE: Dirk makes a quick break for the hidden dock at the base of the cliff on the Bayside of the Safe House. He makes the dock, but Petra's gone. Dirk fumbles for his Radio Cell, but it's not there. Maybe he lost it when he low crawled.

He digs for his cell and finds it, then speed dials Pieter, speaking quietly in Dutch.

"It's me, Standby One."

Dirk quietly moves to a defensive spot overlooking the dock and checks his perimeter - Three-Hundred-Sixty.

PIETER'S HOUSE - OTROBANDA: Pieter responds back in Dutch.

"Dirk. . .Derrick and I can extract you. Just hold THERE . . . Over!"

SAFE HOUSE - BAYSIDE: Dirk answers in Dutch.

"Good, maybe we can do it by boat. I'm at the south side of the SAFE HOUSE DOCK at 100 meters, look for my laser.

I'll go red three, then switch to solid green. Make it quick and be ready for anything. These guys are super lethal. OUT!"

The PREDITOR at Sea, North of Curacao

Chapter 14: THIEL DEEP DIVE FACILITY

UNDERWATER DIVE FACILITY: Newport Bay on the Southeast shore of Curacao is the home of ZAAN THIEL, a fifty something combination playboy and professor look alike. ZAAN stands watching Nick's Super Yacht arrival. Inside his facility are two surprisingly small Commercial Bathyspheres. Both are suspended by ceiling lifts, side by side over an internal moon-pool. The Pool has under building access to the nearby Bay.

Two other people besides ZAAN are MILLING ABOUT AND CHATTING in the facility as Nick's Crew dock the High Tech Yacht, PREDITOR.

Nick disembarks and makes an entrance with his FIRST MATE ROLF, following silently behind him with a five-inch deep briefcase in one hand. ZAAN looks at both of them with a skeptical expression, then speaks directly to Nick with a strong Dutch accent.

"Jon tells me that you need one of my BEEBES! So, what are you up to these days?"

"Can't exactly say. . . but, what's it going to take to borrow one of them for the day?"

"Last time that happened, Nick, we ended up with over Three-Thousand in damages due to your driver's negligence.

You really pissed off the PROFESSOR on that one."

"That Guy's gone, ZAAN! And it will Never happen again, My Friend."

"So, convince me, Nick!"

"Come on, ZAAN, You've got the only GAME in town. . . Here's the deal. Not Only, do we use your man, *'The Professor'*, to drive it. But we'll pay for you to use your own BOAT, to Ferry it out to our coordinates."

Without any hesitation, ZAAN reacts. . .

"Up front that's Ten-Thousand US$ for a full day with both, Nick. You got that on you?"

"It's a big Salvage Job. . . and the money's 'a-flow'n, ZAAN."

"Yeah, yours came in six months late last time; and cost me a ton of interest, Nick."

Nick snaps his fingers, and Rolf moves up beside him with the brief case.

Nick opens it in front of ZAAN -- it's
stashed with US$ One-Hundred
denomination Bill Packs, as Nick grabs
TWO Packs and holds it up.

"Here's Five-Thousand US$ to get us
started."

Nick hands ZAAN the cash, with a hand
written note from Dirk. Rolf closes the
briefcase then moves back behind Nick.

"And the Note's the drop Coordinates.
I'll call you on the ACTUAL GOTO
coordinates, when we get in position."

ZAAN takes the cash and carefully looks
over the bundled Packs, then reads the
note from Dirk with the Coordinates. .
.

Still suspicious, he looks up at Nick.

"You know THESE are inside the
Exclusion Zone the Coast Guard has been
broadcasting on the Marine Safety Band
over the last few hours. They want
everyone clear of ST. JORIS and THE
BLUE WALL. . . Why?"

"That's for us, ZAAN. It's a TOP SECRET
PLAN and all that, you know. . .

And we'll need your BEEBE with the
'remote hands' on it, not that Tourist
Viewing Toy you've been renting out to
those Rich Americans. Plus, ZAAN, we
could be down to Two-Thousand depending
on our target."

"Look Nick, this sounds well beyond what I can offer you. Besides, that water over there is the deepest and most dangerous on this island.

I've got major safety concerns, too. My BEEBE could get smashed into that deep rock wall in an instant. No one could save those guys, at a Thousand or more Meters. . ."

Undaunted, Nick again looks back at Rolf and motions for him to open the briefcase. This time he takes out four more Packs of bills totaling Ten-Thousand US$ Dollars.

"Here's some more Insurance Money to keep us honest!"

Nick hands ZAAN the additional cash packets.

"And, if the current is too rough down there, we'll abort with 'No Refund' –

You'll keep it all!"

Finally satisfied, ZAAN grins at Nick.

"Okay, Nick. . . We're a GO on this one, just keep me informed all along the way."

OUTSIDE THE HIGH TECH YACHT: In moments, Nick and Rolf are exiting ZAAN's Facility and heading for the boarding ramp of PREDITOR.

They both see Petra and her dog Wolf on the dock as they begin boarding. Petra is just finishing tying off her JETBOAT next to the stern of the Yacht.

Nick sends Rolf to the BRIDGE, while he and two crew members urgently rush down to help Petra, Jon and Jennifer unload.

Jon looks stressed out, as Nick addresses him in Dutch.

"Where's Dirk? What happened over there, Jon?"

"All Hell broke loose, Nick! They found the SAFE HOUSE and started shooting."

Nick immediately turns to Petra who's bending over to gather her gear, exposing a 38mm Auto Glock stuffed in the back of her pants.

"So where IS Dirk, Petra?"

Petra responds casually without looking up.

"He's okay, I'm sure. We plotted fields of fire in advance. He knew how to take them out. He wanted to cover our escape!"

Then she stands up, to face Nick with a confident assassin's grin on her face.

"Besides, he had his Night-Vision Sniper Rifle with six magazines. That should be enough to take out 'Hezbollah'."

Suddenly, Petra's cell begins BUZZING LOUDLY. She grabs it and turns away from everyone speaking faintly. No one hears her.

PIETER'S FAMILY LANDHOUSE: Dirk's on his cell to Petra. . .

"The situation got worse, Petra, but I'm Okay. Staying at Pieter's Dad's LANDHOUSE. I'm going back in to OTROBANDA soon, so I'll need to hear what Jennifer's dug up."

OUTSIDE THE PREDITOR YACHT: Petra turns to Jennifer - then gives a thumbs-up to everyone.

"He's alright."

Jennifer urgently runs back to Petra, as Petra hands off her cell to Jennifer.

"He needs to talk to you."

PIETER'S FAMILY LANDHOUSE: Dirk smooths out his voice from 'War Mode' as he tries to calm Jennifer on his cell. . .

"Things are fine, Kiddo. . . Hey, that work you did for me, I'm proud of you for that.

How did it turn out?"

OUTSIDE THE PREDITOR YACHT: Jennifer's almost in tears, as she emotionally freezes.

Then she gets serious again, as she speaks confidently into Petra's Cell.

"Our greatest immediate adversary is definitely 'The Banque Du Curacao'.

And more significantly, the local Security Force controlled by its Director, Henrik VANBOVEEN."

She hesitates and adds. . .

"Do you need to know how to find him?"

PIETER'S FAMILY LANDHOUSE: Dirk assured but powerful voice calms her. . .

"No, Kiddo. But VANBOVEEN and his Bank are a serious force to deal with. We've got to find some inside support in the Government, if we want to tackle those Guys.

Listen, Jennifer, I need to talk to Jon."

OUTSIDE THE PREDITOR YACHT: Jennifer finally lights with up a smile of true satisfaction, drying her tears, as she calls Jon to hand off the cell. But he's standing right beside her as their eyes meet.

"He needs your help now, Jon."

Jon quickly takes the Cell . . .

"How can I help, Dirk?"

PIETER'S FAMILY LANDHOUSE: Dirk's voice returns back to 'War Mode' to get Jon's attention. . .

"Get the Professor and convince ZAAN how bad we need that Special BEEBE."

OUTSIDE THE PREDITOR YACHT: Jon is serious, but concerned as he answers. . .

"The Professor hasn't shown up yet, but I'll call his place and get him in here."

PIETER'S FAMILY LANDHOUSE: Dirk's voice turns URGENT. . .

"Good. But make it quick, this situation is developing fast, Jon.

Now, let me sign off with Petra."

OUTSIDE THE PREDITOR YACHT: Jon waves Petra back to the phone handing it off, then uses his own cell to dial the Professor.

"He needs you, Petra."

Petra grins back taking the cell, as Jon gets NO ANSWER on his cell call.

"How do we take it from here, Dirk?"

PIETER'S FAMILY LANDHOUSE: Dirk's voice remains energized . . .

"Let's put Jon and Nick in on this call too! Get some place Private and use your Speaker Mode. I want to build a serious Plan that can take these Bastards that Jennifer discovered down, once and for all. . . Now that I know who they are!"

OUTSIDE THE HIGH TECH YACHT: Petra grabs her Weapons Rucksack and motions to Jon and Nick, as she starts toward the Yacht ramp entrance.

"Jon, Nick, we need some place PRIVATE!"

Nick jumps ahead of Petra, as they all move upward toward the bridge of the Yacht. He then turns back to First Mate Rolf, with orders in COMMAND mode.

"Rolf, get Jennifer safely stowed in my stateroom. Then cast off for our coordinates on the North Coast."

ROLF instantly reacts . . .

"Aye, Captain. . . Full Ahead?"

"Aye Rolf, Full Ahead, Flank Speed!"

The PREDITOR YACHT Crew jumps into action and buttons up the ship, as ZAAN's dock team casts off her ropes.

Smoothly, the streamlined beauty moves away from the wharf and flashes her stainless steel in the bright morning sunlight as Rolf begins RAMPING UP her turbines.

Only the ENGINES MUTED HIGH PITCHED WHINE can be HEARD as the PREDITOR quickly clears the harbor, almost wakeless, moving North Eastward toward its new destination.

Chapter 15: BANQUE TRANSMISSION ROOM

BANQUE DU CURACAO - TRANSMISSION ROOM:
We enter the International Wire
Transfer Room in the Security Compound
Section near Henrik's Office. Two Bank
Operations Clerks are quickly flipping
transaction screens on computer
monitors with multi-million dollar
financial transactions on screen. Funds
are being wire transferred in and out
of various worldwide accounts.

Hendrik VANBOVEEN enters and stares
intently at details on one of the
screens, as he goes to the female
Clerk's keyboard and addresses her in
Dutch.

"Set up an encrypted data transfer to
Berne for me, I'll handle the Note."

The female Clerk types several codes
into her keyboard, then gets up from
her computer console. Hendrik sits down
at her keyboard.

"I'll takes it from here and send it
myself. You two, take a coffee break."

Both Clerks respond in unison without
reaction.

"Yes, Sir!"

As the Clerks leave the room, Hendrik begins typing infinite details of the events on the Island that have taken place up to that moment.

Once the information packet is complete, he sends it, SECURELY to Chairman VORT BLAAU at the Bank's Headquarters in Berne, Switzerland.

He then TRASHES the computer document file he created and walks out of the Transmission Room to his own office.

Moments later, one of the two clerks returns with coffee in hand. She purposely spills some on her keyboard. The System reacts by shutting down.

The other clerk -- an older male -- enters.

Observing what appears to be an accident, he's seething his Dutch, but just loud enough to show extreme anger, not enough to be heard outside the room.

"OMIGOD, what have you done, ANNE! They'll kill you, YOU Idiot! We're never supposed to have Coffee in here."

Anne reacts in fear, crying for his mercy in English.

"I wasn't thinking, HANS. He always makes me nervous. What can we do?"

Hans suddenly tries to empathize with her plight, as he responds more gently in English. She is of course, a beautiful young Girl, he would someday love to BANG!

"There's only one solution without rebooting the whole Bank Wide System.

It's really illegal, but no one knows the old tricks around here, like I do. They've just never paid much attention to me.

And they've never paid me enough money, to really help them."

Anne is finally smiling - he's under her spell.

"So WHAT are you talking about doing, Hans?"

Hans is intense . . .

"We can pull the back-up command module and re-load the data from the last hour from that. Then just not send it, since it's already transmitted. Then we'll erase everything that was either confidential or unneeded."

You retrieve and I'll re-boot the local system CPU. Just remember, everything has to be aligned down to the last microsecond."

Hans exits to the CPU closet and in moments, Anne has Henrik's secure transmission on a flash drive. Then silently, she slips it into her purse and begins cleaning the confidential and unneeded data from her screens.

SECRET ISRAELI BANK - ZURICH, SWITZERLAND:

Agents for the ISRAELI MOSSAD have been scanning a battery of Bank Transaction Monitors for potential Bullion related incidents WORLDWIDE, for hours.

But more critically, they have just received a Document from a Deep Agent, revealing that something is in play between the Banque Du Curacao and its Headquarters in Berne, Switzerland.

A Director enters into the Office Suite. He's agitated.

One of his Operatives speaking with a German accent, motions for him, as he urgently looks at his screen.

"ARRI, we have something here."

ARRI in an Israeli accent, controls his reaction to NEUTRAL.

"When did you receive this?"

Swiftly the Operative responds . . .

"It's been flowing out of Curacao all night.

We've had this Bank in Berne, Switzerland on the WATCH LIST here for over a year. This is the first time we've gotten this much Intel on the HIMMLER GOLD Cover-up, but this Branch is feeding it in from Curacao."

ARRI demands. . .

"Who do we have in Berne?"

Again the Operative responds . . .

"No one yet, but ISSER and Yuval, Level One Mossad arrived here from Paris this evening. They're inside now!"

ARRI reacts back. . .

"Who do we have on that Island?"

The Operative is stumped. . .

"Agents immediately on the ground. . . Well?"

The Operative - clearly frustrated - looks at ARRI.

"No One."

ARRI snaps back. . .

"What about SAYANIM, Back-up or other friends?"

The Operative looks lost in thought . . .

"Well, maybe a Dutch Special Forces OP
. . . He's retired, although a proven
Zionist! Part of the Joint Forces
Operation Netherlands loaned us during
the Gulf War."

Again ARRI barks back. . .

"How is he rated, then?"

The Operative feeds in another thought
. . .

"He's SAYANIM of sorts, a support
agent, but a non-Jew . . . a 'need to
know only' type!"

Finally, ARRI makes his decision. . .

"Okay. Contact him and have him set up
Cars, a SAFE HOUSE and a Pick-up at
their Airport. No details, just have
him 'Wait for Contact', ONLY."

ARRI then adds. . .

"Have Mikala set up a Jet and a KIDON
Squad from Tel Aviv. I want them there,
early tomorrow! And redirect ISSER and
Yuval to Berne, but first to my office,
Now."

ARRI leaves abruptly, as the FIRST and
SECOND Operatives begin cell and land-
line calls to various contacts.

One is to DIRK VAN DER ROO's contact
number.

The FIRST Operative is on the monitor scanning names and addresses in Curacao, then makes the call in Dutch.

"Is this Hotel Kura HULANDA?"

HOTEL KURA HULANDA — CURACAO: Cell contact is made with a Dutch receptionist at a Hotel address in OTROBANDA, Curacao.

"Mister VAN DER ROO's Office . . . Can I be of service."

Chapter 16: BANQUE DU CURAÇAO HDQTRS.

HEADQUARTERS - BANQUE DU CURAÇAO - BERNE, SWITZERLAND: A Secret Vault-Like Transaction Room within the Bank with several video monitors - Four frames on each, with Financials streaming. A Clearing Clerk working transactions at a keyboard — Plus, a dedicated monitor, facing the Clerk with an individual ON SCREEN . . .

ON SCREEN: VORT BLAAU - BLAAU in German accented English.

"What is our current system wide GOLD BULLION inventory?"

The Clearing Clerk responds, in a matter of fact tone, with a German accent. Almost aloof to the fact it's BLAAU.

"Sir, we are currently at Forty-Thousand Troy-Ounces in 400 oz. London Standard Bars Current Value at today's Spot:

Four-Point-Six BILLION US Dollars.

And Four-Thousand Troy-Ounces in Euro Kilogram Bars - Current Value at today's Spot:

Four-Hundred-Eleven MILLION US
Dollars."

ON SCREEN: Again, BLAAU in German
accented English.

"So, we are at nearly FIVE BILLION US
Dollars in all our Banks. . .

So at today's Spot. . . WHAT would One-
Hundred tons calculate to?"

The Clearing Clerk remains in silence -
then a sudden GASP of surprise . . .

"Is the TONNAGE broken into Four-
Hundred Troy-Ounce London Standard
Bars, Sir?"

ON SCREEN: BLAAU in accented English. .
.

"No, it's Ten Kilogram Bars."

The Clearing Clerk responds quietly . .
.

"That's unusual, Sir. . . Are they
Swiss?"

ON SCREEN: BLAAU is now irritated, as
he reacts, belligerently. . .

"NO, they're GERMAN Bars!"

Just calculate them at the same RATE,
as London Standard Bars!"

The Clearing Clerk senses BLAAU's irritation and finally responds, to avoid a confrontation.

ON SCREEN: BLAAU's no longer aloof ON SCREEN, his face is contorted.

The Clearing Clerk answers as best he can.

"That could create a transfer/reconciliation problem, Sir."

ON SCREEN: BLAAU further irritated . . .

"Just do IT, you imbecile. . . And NEVER, question my authority!"

The Clearing Clerk becomes very nervous, responds softly.

"Yes Sir, just give me a moment."

He CHOKES LOUDLY. . .

"It would clear at slightly over One-Hundred-Three Million US Dollars per Ton - Or, TEN-POINT-THREE BILLION US Dollars Total."

ON SCREEN: Without notice, BLAAU clicks-off. The SCREEN goes blank.

BANQUE DU CURAÇAO, EXECUTIVE OFFICES - BERNE: An elaborate Executive Office - VORT BLAAU is sorting through notes from a recent secure Transmission - reading intently.

BLAAU presses a button - His Secretary enters the room from a side door - He reacts - very serious in German.

"Get me Henrik on the secure line.

And, what's the time there?"

His Secretary looks at her two arm watches, speaks German.

"Yes, Sir!

It's just after Seven PM Atlantic Time, there."

BLAAU reacts somewhat satisfied. . .

"Good! Hurry then."

The Secretary exits. A moment later his phone rings as she announces the CALL.

"Sir! Henrik is on the line."

CURACAO: Henrik responding in English.

BLAAU: Irritated as he speaks. . .

"Okay, Okay! Listen to me. There's a change of plans for you and your people, Henrik.

I've contacted that Oil Drilling Subsidiary we bought in Aruba last year."

CURACAO: Henrik again responding in English.

BLAAU: Acknowledges Henrik . . .

"Yes, that's the one. Lagos Ltd.

They have a Semi-Submersible Drilling Rig with Deep Water Repair Divers and Equipment positioned near Northwest Curacao off the Bay of Venezuela.

I'm having them pull operations and move that unit to just off the entrance to ST. JORIS BAY."

CURACAO: Henrik responds in English.

BLAAU: Again irritated . . .

"No, they don't need a TUG. It's self-propelled at over Seven-Knots, and it will be there tomorrow -- by afternoon, late.

So, here's what you've got to do, immediately! Contact your friend in the Governor's Office and get us a backdated Twenty Year Oil Lease for a Ten-Kilometer Drilling Zone off that Bay."

CURACAO: Henrik excitedly responds.

BLAAU: He's frustrated with Henrik . .

"I don't CARE! Make it two to three years back, but be sure it's Restricted and can be Enforced by the Dutch Coast Guard, as long as we need them."

CURACAO: Henrik responds in English.

BLAAU: Suddenly, he's seriously irritated.

"Start handing out money THEN. . . YOU MORON! Even ECO Terrorists need money! This thing's almost three times as big as OUR current Asset level!

You've got no time to waste. By controlling the Drill-Zone, we can enforce a 'Complete Information Blackout' of that area.

We can even keep those Locals out of ST. JORIS BAY itself. That way, your Security Team can keep eyes & bodies out of there. . . while we finish the job."

CURACAO: Henrik goes quiet. . .

BLAAU: BLAAU's finally satisfied. . .

"Okay then, Henrik, get it done, RIGHT this time! And make me Proud of you, once again, Old Fellow!"

CURACAO: Henrik is without comment. . .

BLAAU: BLAAU SLAMS the receiver down for effect as they go OFF-AIR!

BLAAU then removes a Monte Cristo cigar from his desk side humidor.

He preps it, then lights up. After a long drag on the cigar, he grins deceitfully, prepares himself a Scotch from his back bar, then makes another call from his private cell phone.

The DCG Cutter ZEELAND at Sea, CURACAO

Chapter 17: NORTH COAST OF CURACAO

NICK'S YACHT — NEAR THE BLUE WALL: It's getting DARK, OVERCAST and WINDY as Nick's SUPER Yacht finally enters the Zone near the dive site.

OVERHEAD an NH-90 German Built Helicopter FLIES by, LOUDLY breaking through the natural sounds of the sea.

In moments, the NH-90 begins landing on a High Tech Dutch Fast Attack Cutter, ZEELAND, idling over One-Thousand Meters out from the entrance to ST. JORIS BAY.

Nick's Yacht slows and begins to drift, only Three-Hundred Meters from the cliff walls at ST JORIS. At once, the Coast Guard radios the Yacht's Command Deck.

YACHT'S BRIDGE VIEW: Four foot SWELLS and WIND are causing some ship movement, as the PREDITOR slows to IDLE. Several crewmembers on the Bridge are working a battery of video screens and High Tech instruments as the First Mate and Nick prepare their Divers for a quick descent to the Blue Wall.

THE DUTCH COAST GUARD VESSEL: The Coast Guard OFFSHORE Commander Radios to the Yacht in Dutch with a routine interrogation request.

"Dutch Super-Yacht PREDATOR, what is your intention?"

YACHT'S BRIDGE: Nick immediately goes to the COMMO-Screen - clicks in his radio headset, then recognizes the Commander and responds in English.

"It's Nick Christiaan here, COMMANDER VISSER. We're on a repair test run of the PREDATOR's engines and hull in rough water.

Hope all is well with You, your wife and family."

THE DUTCH COAST GUARD VESSEL: VISSER responds equally friendly, now in accented English.

"Ah Yes. And it's hoped to hear YOU are well today, Nick."

VISSER then adds in a more serious tone. . .

"Nick, the Admiral has temporarily placed these waters, off ST. JORIS, into a Ten Kilometer Restricted Zone. . .

You will need to Test the PREDATOR further out or in another area off the island."

YACHT'S BRIDGE: Nick needing more time, mutes his COMMO-Microphone and indicates by hand MOVEMENT to his First Mate; 'All Stop'.

"Will Comply, Commander, however we have a slight vibration problem on our Starboard Propulsion Jet."

Nick tries to get back to a friendly tone.

"Can you give us some time to fix it, MIKE?"

THE DUTCH COAST GUARD VESSEL: Commander VISSER responds, but still with an official voice.

"Nick, we can ONLY allow twenty minutes for that, or Under Sanction we'll have to board or tow YOU.

YACHT'S BRIDGE: Nick quickly responds .
. .

"That's good, Mike, That's good!

We'll Comply - Out."

Nick RUSHES off the Bridge down to the Underwater Access Room below the stern of the Yacht.

THE YACHT'S DIVE MOON-ROOM: Four foot swells LOUDLY SPLASH WAVES into the Dive MOON-ROOM.

Nick enters quickly making sure his two
Deep Water JIM Suited Divers are sealed
in their atmospheric dive suits and
ready. The JIM DIVERS mount their high
speed motorized transporter.

Jon and Jennifer have also just arrived
into the Moon Room to observe the
operation, as Nick plugs in his radio
headset and puts the MIC on SPEAKER
MODE.

Although, the Yacht is stationary, the
intense swells outside continue to
SPLASH SEA WATER around the room's Dive
Opening.

Nick is tense and urgent, knowing time
is short for them. . .

"Is everything Ready down here?"

Both Divers nod 'OKAY' as Jon
immediately jumps into the
conversation. . .

"Nick, there's a problem! I can't reach
the Professor. I've called Dirk to make
a run by his Apartment, but ZAAN won't
let me operate the Beebe alone. . .

Only the Professor's skills can take on
THE BLUE WALL with that special remote
Beebe."

"Well keep me updated, Jon . . . For
now, though, we've got a Coast Guard
Cutter upstairs and they want us out of
here, Fast!"

Out of the blue, DIVER ONE's voice shouts out of Nick's RADIO SPEAKER in accented English. . .

"JESUS, Nick! This Dive alone is twenty minutes. With positioning adjustments we're at least an HOUR down. How are we going to work this?"

Nick yells back to the RADIO SPEAKER . . .

"I've got a Plan, you GUYS! Just follow the preset guidelines we've already worked out and FIND that U-Boat. Besides, No Decompression and No Narcosis with these new JIM suits. We'll be right here when you come up!"

Again, Jon jolts into the fray . . .

"Hey Nick, was that Mike over there on the DUTCH Cutter?"

Nick laughs, then smiles back at Jon . . .

"Yeah, it's Him alright. But this time he's got, a serious Cobb up his Ass, 'THE ADMIRAL'. . .And we can't get around it! The damn Admiral has put a Ten Kilometer Restriction Zone on ST. JORIS."

Abruptly, Jennifer comments . . .

"Those Bastards at the Banque Du Curacao got to him, I'm sure.

When I was online, I noticed the political appointments their Bank has influenced over the years here on the island. That Admiral's position is not DUTCH Defense Department, it's a Political appointment. In fact, he's not even a member of the Dutch Navy. He's a local Judge. And I'll bet Henrik VANBOVEEN owns him."

INSIDE THE DIVE MOON-POOL: The Divers hit the turbulent sea water, launch the high speed motorized transporter craft, and mount it. Then submerge completely in moments, as Nick comes over to Jennifer and Jon.

Meanwhile, OTTO, the Dive Boss urgently speaks in Dutch, as he begins a COMMO-Check with the Divers.

"Descend, Descend! Clear, to One-Hundred Meters and HOLD."

The Dive Boss's VOICE trails off into the background, as he instructs them to descend BEYOND One-Hundred Meters.

DEEP OPEN OCEAN - OFF THE BLUE WALL: We are now visually following both Divers riding on the high speed motorized transporter as they move down into black ocean depths to the drop-off.

CRYSTAL 'GIN-CLEAR' WATER surrounds them with masses of various sized fish, along with brilliant coral outcrops are visible below them.

At once, the Diver's and Transporter's Lights flash-on, as they begin descending away from the surface light penetration of the Moon Pool.

Slowly, they glide below the first thermocline into the great dark depths toward the possible U-Boat's graveyard.

THE YACHT'S DIVE MOON-ROOM: SWELLS SPLASH continuously in the background from the Moon-Pool as Nick starts heading to the Bridge, while he finishes talking to Jennifer and Jon.

"That's good information to know about the Admiral, Jennifer, but basically were screwed unless we can get more time on the surface here. And all this, has eaten up at least fifteen solid minutes.

For now, I've got to get back to the Bridge and see if we can keep MIKE from boarding us."

"Nick, Mike VISSER has been my personal friend, since I came to Curacao. Let me talk to him and see if we can get some more time."

Nicks hesitates. . .

"Okay THEN, Jon . . . You two come with me! I'll fill you in on what's happening.

Let's get up to the Bridge."

Nick, Jon, and Jennifer exit the Moon-Room Dive Bay, while the Dive Boss continues his COMMO COMMANDS with both his Divers.

SEA SOUNDS fade into the background, as Nick SLAMS the watertight door, LOCKING AND SEALING it, behind them.

YACHT'S BRIDGE: The Yacht's engines are at All Stop.

Some WAVE ACTION and WIND is moving the Yacht, even with the position stabilizer motors working overtime. Nick enters the Command Bridge with Jon and Jennifer in tow.

Rolf, the First Mate is TALKING INDISTINCTLY to the engine room. Several crewmembers are working video screens and stabilizer controls, as Jon again speaks up.

"Nick, do you know if this Yacht has any Kitesurfing Gear?"

"What do you have in mind, Jon?"

"I trained Mike to Kitesurf. He loves it. Jennifer and I could distract him for a short while, if you've got some gear. Maybe he'll even join us . . . He's crazy like that!"

Nick caught by surprise, 'LAUGHS' OUT LOUD!

"Nick, he once anchored his Cutter while on Duty, over at Jan Thiel Beach and joined us for several hours.

Of course there were no Emergency calls, but he would have broken off, if one came up. Give me a chance to test him. The water out there's a bit rough, but it's a great time to do it with this wind staying steady."

Nick again chuckles, then quizzically looks over at Rolf.

"Do we have any of that gear on board this play toy, Rolf?"

"I inventoried four Kites and four Boards with support gear in the Aft Ski-Doo-Watercraft Bay last week, Captain."

"Then get 'em down there and get 'em Suited-up, Rolf."

Jon is still a bit apprehensive . . .

"But, I've still got to make sure Mike likes the idea, Nick?"

"Okay, then. Here goes, Jon! You're on, Kiddo."

Nick speaks Dutch into the hand-held Inter-Ship COMMO-MIC.

"Super-Yacht PREDATOR to Coast Guard Cutter ZEELAND, Over!"

THE DUTCH COAST GUARD VESSEL: A ZEELAND Crewman acknowledges in a Dutch military tone.

YACHT'S BRIDGE: Nick speaks Dutch . . .

"Requesting Commander VISSER, Over!"

THE DUTCH COAST GUARD VESSEL: After a short delay Commander VISSER responds in Dutch.

YACHT'S BRIDGE: Switching to English, Nick implores his friend cautiously. .

"We're still running TESTS, Mike. But, I've got someone here, who desperately wants to talk to you!"

Jon enthusiastically takes over the Microphone as Nick steps over to quietly confide with his First Mate.

"It's me, MIKE -- It's Jon!"

THE DUTCH COAST GUARD VESSEL: Commander VISSER immediately recognizes the voice.

"Jon . . . What are you doing over there on that Super-Yacht?"

YACHT'S BRIDGE: Jon is animated as he speaks. . .

"I've known Nick for quite some time!

When he told me he was coming out here
for Test Runs, I asked him if Jennifer
and I could catch the wind here and
sail around the ST. JORIS INLET, while
he was out here.

We've got plenty of boards, Mike. Why
don't you come over and join us!"

THE DUTCH COAST GUARD VESSEL: Commander
VISSER 'LAUGHES' – Then becomes
serious.

"Oh, I couldn't do that. Besides I'm on
duty, Jon."

YACHT'S BRIDGE: Jon's response is
spirited –

"Haa'ah, that's never stopped you
before, Mike!"

THE DUTCH COAST GUARD VESSEL: Commander
VISSER seems somber as he speaks –

"Well, this is serious business today.
The Admiral sent us down here with
strict orders.

YACHT'S BRIDGE: Jon continues egging
him on with his feisty teasing –

"You're here, aren't you! What more do
they want. . . Besides, this boat's out
for the moment and they need more time
to get it up and running . . . That's
plenty of time for us to make a few
runs out here 'til sunset."

THE DUTCH COAST GUARD VESSEL: Commander
VISSER seems more relaxed as he
listens.

"I can't change out of Uniform on this
one, Jon . . . Tell you what, though. .
. You and Jennifer can do it.

I'll give you an extra hour. But as
soon as that sunset hits, You and Nick
need to be out of here!"

YACHT'S BRIDGE: Jon continues his
playful attitude -

"I'll take it, Mike. But Jennifer wants
to stop over to see you on our last run
. . ."

THE DUTCH COAST GUARD VESSEL: Commander
VISSER again, LAUGHS out loud -

"I don't know if I can hold the CREW
under CONTROL, if 'Beautiful' Jennifer
comes on board!

But, I can't wait to see you both,
Out!"

YACHT'S BRIDGE: Jon and Jennifer are
smiling and silently making victory
MOTIONS with their arms in the air.
They both BOLT out of the BRIDGE with
Rolf, down to the Ski-Doo-Bay to get
fitted in their Kitesurfing gear and
out onto the waves.

Nick immediately contacts Otto on his
headset for the DIVERS status.

"Where are they?"

THE YACHT'S DIVE MOON-ROOM: Otto responds back to Nick in accented English. . .

"They're below Two-Hundred Meters and the water temp has dropped to thirty-seven degrees Fahrenheit or three degrees Celsius.

They've found a ledge. It extends away from the Blue Wall about five meters, but the deeper they go, the wider the ledge gets.

DEEP OPEN OCEAN - OFF THE BLUE WALL: We are now visually following both Divers as they enter the ABYSS. The Submersible Transporter moves them deeper down the ledge of THE BLUE WALL. The water is still clear, but much darker, as their HALOGEN LIGHTS are CRITICAL. Infrequently they see major sized Grouper and twenty-foot long Sharks, as they pass by rocky Outcrops. They are now forty minutes into the Dive.

All, but blue and black colors have left the light spectrum as the HALOGENS pierce the dark water out to Twenty-Five meters. They continue descending slowly, as they enter the fifth thermocline. But at Three Hundred meters the ledge begins to narrow and drops off again into an even deeper abyss.

Suddenly, a dark outline begins to form below them, as DIVER ONE begins his COMMO Transmission to Otto. . .

"We are less than seven minutes before assent -- Water Temp is one degree Celsius.

A Dark object below us, on the ledge . . .

Our Visual is reduced to twenty meters!

Wait One . . .

The stern of what looks like a U-Boat hangs Five to Ten meters precariously over that narrow ledge. It's partially broken away from the hull, AFT of the Conning Tower.

Conning Tower has a Viking Ship with Dragon Prow and numbered markings.

Wait One . . .

Numbers are U-1055"

YACHT'S BRIDGE: Nick gets the relay, then gives URGENT orders to Otto.

"That's Great News, Otto! Have them look into the opening with their Power-Mag HALOGENS!

But don't enter that hull or even touch the walls of that broken structure. . . it might collapse or break off."

DEEP OPEN OCEAN - OFF THE BLUE WALL:
Finally, we can see U-Boat-1055 as
Diver Two positions the Submersible
Transporter with all Lights directed
into the broken hull wall.

YACHT'S BRIDGE: After a long silence,
Nick SCREAMS back to Otto!

"What do they see in there?

Tell me Otto. . . Tell me?"

DEEP OPEN OCEAN - OFF THE BLUE WALL:
Both Divers are spellbound, as they
look into the interior.

"There's a body. A WWII U-Boat Crewman
in a KRIEGSMARINE Uniform. His entire
arm has been severed at the shoulder.
This freezing water must have
maintained his flesh intact, but now
it's deteriorating fast since it's
exposed to the elements and possibly
these scavengers we keep seeing. Large
Grouper and Bull Sharks.

This crack in the hull must be recent.

There appears to be a rock slide from
the WALL that damaged the boat and
caused this HULL break.

Wait One!"

YACHT'S BRIDGE: Nick again yells to his
Dive Boss, Otto.

"For God's sake, Man . . .

What do they see in there?"

DEEP OPEN OCEAN - OFF THE BLUE WALL: U-1055 — THE AFT TORPEDO ROOM OPENING. Diver TWO moves off the Transporter and climbs almost fully into the opening. His Power Mag HALOGEN Lamps beaming at high intensity.

Without warning, a massive Black Moray Eel moves out of the opening, as the Diver back kicks to avoid its open jaws. Quickly, Diver TWO motions violently to his rear, to Diver ONE.

"Watch Out, Peter!"

The Eel comes right at Peter's face, then moves down the ledge into deeper water, as its tail strokes his sealed JIM gear unit.

Peter follows its movement with his lights until it disappears, then reacts on COMMO.

"That was too close for comfort. Can you see around that Crewman's body, Bakker?"

Diver TWO stays almost in the opening with his Lights on.

"Yes, there are many wooden crates strewn around the flooring deck and one is broken open.

It appears to be filled with Metal Ingots. The Ingot surface is shiny, but blackened.

Wait One!"

Peter calls out URGENT. . .

"Time is up, Bakker! Hey Otto, we really need a Bathysphere for this Deep Work!

. . . We need more time on site, too!"

Diver TWO moves back onto the Transporter, as he shouts into his COMMO.

"We are Now Ready to Ascend, Otto!

Preparing for Ascent . . . Re-Positioning NOW. Out."

COMMO transmissions end, as the Dive team begins their Ascent Plan, up to the Yacht's Moon Room.

Chapter 18: THE KITESURF DISTRACTION

NICK'S YACHT — BRIDGE: The Yacht
PREDATOR is still at ALL STOP, while
Crewmen work the various High Tech
control panels and Hull Thrusters to
keep the Yacht in position, as Otto
finishes his conversation with the
Captain.

"Did you get all that, Nick!"

"Thanks, Otto. I think we know what the
situation is now. Bring them up safely
and contact me when they arrive in the
Dive Bay. I need a complete debriefing.

PREDITOR — OUTSIDE FORWARD DECK: Nick
immediately leaves the Bridge and
checks the open Ocean conditions. They
are now positioned at a location half
the distance between the DUTCH Coast
Guard Cutter and the BLUE WALL.

WAVES RUSH LOUDLY by the YACHT with
white caps and strong winds pushing
them sideways. In the Western Sky, the
Sun is setting, but it's still bright
enough as he watches Jon and Jennifer
Kitesurfing in parallel toward the
Coast Guard Cutter. They are about to
finish their run.

He can see that the ZEELAND's Coast Guard Crew are making preparations to send a TENDER out to assist Jon and Jennifer in capturing their big ballooned-out Rigid Kites.

THE DUTCH COAST GUARD VESSEL: Commander VISSER, stands on deck watching the Kite-surfers, as he focuses his binoculars on Jon.

At once, Jon makes two high flips, then a helicopter spin in a circle around the CG Cutter.

THE DUTCH COAST GUARD TENDER: Jennifer simply moves in close to the TENDER, so the crew can help pull her Ram Foil Kite down.

She's aboard first, controlling her bidirectional surfboard right onto the TENDER's stern with the help of a crew member. She gives him a big smile, as she takes off her harness and her Kayak Style Life Vest, exposing her curvaceous string bikini clad body. Jennifer then unbuckles her vest, with all the TENDER Crew's eyes on her and yells out.

"Thanks, Boys! Those waves were awesome. Did you see my flips?"

One of the CG Crewman gingerly takes Jennifer's harness and vest from her, while handing her a dry towel and looking her over. He's obviously excited and blushing as he remarks. . .

"I couldn't take my eyes off you. You were incredible out there! How do you like that short Bi-Board you're using?"

Jennifer smiles seductively to him. . .

"You Kitesurf?"

"Yeah, a little over at Blue Bay, Miss."

Jennifer comes back. . .

"It's the only way to go for flips and wind control with that big Ram Foil Kite.

But, my personal board's at home. It's longer. This is the one they loaned me from the Yacht. . . A little more, High Tech."

She crouches quickly, as she spots Jon . . .

"Hey, Look out!"

Jennifer laughs and looks up in nervous excitement. Jon's flying in, then over the TENDER for another pass.

"We'd better catch his Kite, before he has to jump your TENDER again!

THE DUTCH COAST GUARD VESSEL ZEELAND: The TENDER Recovery Ramp is now filled with Crew Members waiting for the TENDER's recovery.

SWELLS and BREAKERS are down to three feet with the WIND SLOWING and QUIETENING. It's Sunset, as a golden light shimmers across the orange sky.

The stern RAMP SLAMS rising. Then falls with the WAVE ACTION. The wind is below twenty knots, but ocean swells still catch the Cutter's up-drift, then drop it several feet, as everyone quickly tries to maintain their footing.

Just as the Crew brings them aboard and stows the TENDER, Mike comes down to greet his friends, smiling as he hugs Jennifer and reaches out to Jon.

"Great Kitesurfing, you two!

You really know how to control that wind with your flips, Jon. And my crew loved it!"

"And Jennifer, you look so happy again. Any new plans?"

"Oh that, Mike?

Can't get him to commit. . .

Just an apartment together, for now!"

Jon 'LAUGH's', as he GRUNTS his perspective.

"And the DOGS, too, Jennifer! That's just like having kids and being married."

Mike 'LAUGH's' with them.

Then he adds. . .

"Well, you've got plenty of time for all that, I'm sure. Come on up to the Bridge, we've got 'HOT Coffee' and I'll show you around. But you can't stay too long . . .

We've got to clear this Zone before nightfall. That's the rules!"

They all head up to the Command Bridge, as the CG Crew completes storing their gear near the TENDER Station, as the Cutter Officially gets back to 'SEA GUARD' Duty.

Chapter 19: THE EXCLUSION ZONE

NICK'S YACHT - LOWER DECK GUEST SUITE:

Outside, STRONGER COASTAL SWELLS continue to cause movement of the Yacht, even with the Stabilizers Holding and Engines at All Stop.

Petra is TALKING INDISTINCTLY in FLUENT CZECH on her Cell Phone as someone KNOCKS on the door to her Suite. Wolf GROWLS, as she motions him into her in-suite bathroom. She closes the door and turns off the cell phone, then immediately lights up a cigarette.

"Who is it?"

It's me, Nick, I'm back."

Petra opens the door as Nick enters. She has the cigarette in her left hand near a Portal. An Ocean wind BLOWS in through the open outside Portal, causing her ash-burn to grow.

"I just got the final debriefing from my Divers. They confirmed that it's the U-1055 and it's got Gold Bullion Ingots in crates all over the inside of the aft torpedo room."

"So what are we up against, Nick?"

"The problem is the boat's stern is projecting five to seven meters over the ledge and that ledge is unstable."

Nick looks around the stateroom at the open outside Portal.

"It's also got a Three-Meter GASH in the HULL just behind the conning tower. That's how they could see inside. The boat could break up with all that dead weight sitting there and sink another Thousand-Meters or more into the Abyss before we can do anything.

We could lose it all, with the slightest shift in that Rock-Wall-Formation, above it.

"I've got to reach Dirk, Nick . . . And get him in on this."

"I know, Petra. PLUS, we need to advise him about the Coast Guard Exclusion Zone. . . They want us out of here by Sunset.

Have you tried to reach him, yet?"

"He hasn't returned my calls and I've left messages at his security office at KURA HULANDA."

Suddenly, Petra's CELL BEGINS BUZZING. It's Dirk returning her call as she answers. . .

"It's great to finally HEAR your Voice, BABE. . . So where have you been?"

SOMEWHERE NEAR OTROBANDA: Dirk's voice is very serious. . .

"Listen Petra, No time for THAT! I got all your TEXT messages about the U-Boat find, but we've got two NEW very CRITICAL problems."

Nick overhears that, as . . .

"SHIT!"

Petra's facial tension shows, as she puts the Call on SPEAKER. . .

"Dirk, I've got Nick here, I'm putting you on SPEAKER! So what have you got?"

SOMEWHERE NEAR OTROBANDA: Dirk is mad. . .

"The Professor's been murdered, Petra . . . and, and . . . The Israelis have just made contact with me, to set up an OPERATION that is designed . . . to probably go after the NAZI GOLD. Somehow they found out this whole situation, is 'IN-PLAY'!

Nick comes visibly unglued, as . . .

"DOUBLE SHIT!"

SOMEWHERE NEAR OTROBANDA: Dirk's urgent. . .

"Listen, BOTH of YOU. . . When we got to the Professor's Apartment we found him with his neck broken. . . Jon's gonna freak-out!"

"What are you talking 'bout, Dirk, I'm freaking out! ZAAN won't let anyone, but the Professor, run that damn Beebe, so now we're all screwed!"

SOMEWHERE NEAR OTROBANDA: Dirk adds. . .

"Get Jon in on this, NOW, Nick!"

"Sorry, Old Man, but he and Jennifer are out distracting his buddy 'Mike', who's running a 'Fully Armed' Coast Guard CUTTER."

SOMEWHERE NEAR OTROBANDA: Dirk again. . . "Then YOU, have to handle this Nick. I've got my hands full with the Israelis! They just contacted me through my Security Office at KURA HULANDA . . . They want me to provide assistance for a large scale operation they're mounting here on Curacao.

"Christ, Dirk. How will all this affect us?"

SOMEWHERE NEAR OTROBANDA: Dirk is intense. "Probably . . . BIG TIME! No details yet, but I'm sure it has to do with YOUR present discovery at the BLUE WALL. . . They've never used my services here on the Island before. . .

Yet, I've been a support operative and advisor for them since the Gulf War."

Petra jumps in . . .

"Well, the good news is, at least we know they're coming, Babe. GOD help, those Bastards they're after!"

Then, Nick jumps in with a sneer in his eyes. . .

"Yeah, Petra! Let's HOPE it's NOT us!"

Another KNOCK on the door of the Suite. It's a Crewman for Nick. . .

As Nick opens the door and urgently SHOUTS back to Petra across the room.

"Petra! I've got to get to the Bridge. Jon and Jennifer have just come aboard and the Coast Guard wants us OUT OF HERE, NOW!

"Go Nick! I'll fill in the details with Dirk . . . See you on the Command Deck."

Petra drops the SPEAKER and goes headset as she returns to Dirk's call.
. .

"Did you hear all that!

SOMEWHERE NEAR OTROBANDA: Dirk softens.
. . "Got It . . . Sounds like you have your hands full, too."

"I have a feeling this is the easy part, Babe. What's coming NEXT may try us all, based on WHAT YOU'RE telling me.

Petra takes a last drag on her cigarette, then tosses it out, as she lights up another.

"Okay, Dirk. Here's what's been going on."

She turns to the in-suite bathroom door and OPENS it, releasing Wolf.

Then moves back to the Portal window, as her VOICE FADES INTO THE BACKGROUND.

The Yacht's turbine engines begin their WHINE, RAMPING-UP and replacing the background SOUNDS OF WIND AND WAVES.

Through Petra's Portal, we can see the final light of DUSK bleaching out from the evaporated sunset, as the Dutch CG Cutter begins disappearing into the far horizon.

PREDITOR's BRIDGE: The Yacht PREDATOR
is now moving rapidly away from the CG
CUTTER ZEELAND, ST. JORIS BAY and THE
BLUE WALL - Eastward to meet ZAAN
Thiel's Deep Diving Ship.

Night Lighting and a distinct lack of
sound or vibration from outside the
CON, contrasts with it's BEEHIVE-LIKE
activity. Crewmembers work a battery of
video screens and instruments as Nick
moves over to TALK with Jon and
Jennifer.

"Jon, we've got to talk, SERIOUS NOW!"

"What's up, Nick?"

"Dirk and his Commando Team found the
Professor at his apartment. He's dead
Jon. Dirk said his neck was broken. He
was murdered."

"OH NO! GAWD Damn. . . I really liked
that guy."

Jennifer quickly grabs him, hugging and
kissing him.

He's too stunned to think, as he just
stares out at the sea. . . she tries to
comfort him. . .

"I'm so SORRY, Babe! It's so Horrible!"

Jon finally reacts. . .

"Who could have done that, Nick, and
WHY? How could they have EVEN known who
he was, in all of this?"

Nick walks over to him and Jennifer, joining the hugs.

"Jon, you've got to pull this together, Son. We've got to beat these bastards. . ."

Nick steps back for a moment to let it all sink in, as he introduces another thought.

"So what did Commander VISSER say, Jon, that got you so concerned, over there?"

Jon hesitates, still stunned by the news of the Professor's MURDER. . .

"Actually, it wasn't exactly 'Mike'."

Nick looks seriously concerned at Jon.

"Who was it, then?"

Jennifer, without thinking, jumps in to fill-in for Jon, who is still in a confused state about the Professor. . .

"What happened, Nick. . . Was, we were all talking about Kitesurfing techniques on his Bridge. . . Then, an urgent call came in from Mike's Admiral. Mike just let us stay on the Bridge, while the COMMO Speaker was LIVE. I'm sure he did it, without realizing, we were all listening."

Finally, Jon chimes in . . .

"Yeah, that was it, Nick. Then, the Admiral started yelling at him.

That they would have to keep ALL surface traffic out of the EXCLUSION ZONE permanently. . . because a Submersible Oil Rig was on its way by tomorrow afternoon."

Nick goes BULLISTIC. . .

"Those Assholes! That really screws us!"

"And he also said, Lagos Oil now has an Official Government Lease on a Ten-Kilometer Exclusion Zone directly over the Blue Wall, including the Entrance and All of ST. JORIS BAY."

Nick is BESERK, as he shouts. . .

"We've got to get this to Dirk! We're going to have to make a completely new plan on how to get that Bullion out. Before those Bastards lock it up.

Time is our worst enemy, now!"

Chapter 20: ZAAN'S BATHYSPHERE (BEEBE)

THE ROTTERDAM - LOWER BOARDING DECK:
It's EARLY Evening as the Navigation
Lights from Nick's Yacht PREDATOR can
be seen in the far distance against the
backdrop of mountain shadows, on the
dark coast of Curacao.

ZAAN Thiel's Deep Water Support Ship,
The ROTTERDAM sits Five-Hundred Meters
offshore.

The Support Ship shifts about
uncomfortably in the Twenty-Knot WIND
and Four-Foot SWELLS, as a Twenty-Five
Foot TENDER arrives from Nick's Yacht.

Jon and Nick climb aboard The
ROTTERDAM, as several crewmen stabilize
their transfer.

Nick waves to ZAAN standing on the
Forward Bridge Deck.

"So what did you find out, Nick? Are we
a Go?"

Nick holds off responding until he and
Jon are face to face with ZAAN on the
BRIDGE DECK -

Nick breathes deeply, almost a sigh . .
.

"Well, not exactly, ZAAN. . ."

He looks to make sure no one is listening - as a NOISY BLOW, MUFFLES their conversation.

"Here's the situation, ZAAN. First, the Coast Guard Commander, who's a bit of an Ally, is patrolling a wide Zone around the BLUE WALL at ST. JORIS and he's keeping all of us out, for now. . .

But he's ONLY working the surface and will not have his Sonar functioning tonight. If we, of course, decide to launch the BEEBE.

ZAAN's facial expression exposes his concern, as he counters. . .

"Before you get too far in all this, Nick, Where's the Professor? You know, I can't let the Beebe dive without Professor Hagen, Nick."

Nick again breathes deeply, with a lament.

"He's not coming, ZAAN. . . Dirk found him at his apartment. . . His neck was broken. He's dead ZAAN, but Jon's his protégé. Jon knows it as well as the Professor.

Jon's ready ZAAN."

ZAAN's face is flushed and stunned, as he reacts.

"He was murdered, wasn't he! There is something 'SINISTER' about all these shenanigans, Nick. You got me in this, up to my eyeballs, too."

Jon almost shouts at him in reaction.

"ZAAN, I CAN do it. . . I'm fully trained as his First Mate and I know it inside and out!"

"And who's going to be YOUR First-Mate, Jon?"

"Jennifer. . . she's been down on it before with me and Hagen. . . Plus, she the fastest computer navigator, I've ever seen. She can blow me and the Professor away, in her recalculations speed."

ZAAN's looks at both Nick and Jon in frustration, as he finally gives in . . .

"Okay, Okay . . . But Good God, Jon . . . That's over Eighteen-Kilometers up the coast from here. The Beebe would be dead-out of battery power, if you added that, plus a Deep Dive to 'Two-Thousand Meters' — a Re-surface -- then a return to our Docking Bay."

Hurriedly, Nick adds his thoughts, and relaxes ZAAN by speaking slower. . .

"Wait . . . wait a minute, ZAAN. Let Jon and I finish. We've sent two ADS Fitted JIM Divers down to our target and it's only Seven-Hundred Meters to that shelf. It's sitting on a Twenty-Meter-Wide outcropping.

Think about that . . . Plus, Jon's Beebe 'down-time' can be kept to a Fifteen Minute Maximum.

All we need is about Two-Hundred-Kilos of material to 'Prove The Site' for a Dutch Maritime Salvage Certificate, and of course a GPS location plot."

ZAAN pulls out a 'hand-held' Downtime & Battery Storage Calculator for the Beebe from his back pocket. He starts punching in numbers.

"Okay, Okay! That's different from what you originally told me, Nick."

Nick holds off the urge to say anything more.

He looks back at the High Tech Saudi Yacht PREDITOR sitting idle in the far distance - lights twinkling in the dark night sky. Then looks back at Jon and grins, as they both watch ZAAN working the numbers.

"God, that Yacht is gorgeous out there, Jon . . . with all those lights glowing."

ZAAN's still looking down at his calculator, serious.

"Okay then, here's the best we can do, Gentlemen.

Somehow, you'll have to get us enough room away from that Coast Guard Cutter to drop off the Beebe. No more than Eight-Kilometers Southeast from the Dive Site.

And, the Beebe can only be down a Maximum of twenty minutes at the actual wreck.

Then, with or without your Two-Hundred-Kilos of wreck material, my Beebe has to surface to the original rendezvous Site – Eight-Kilometers Southeast. And The Rotterdam has to be there, to capture them in the Dive Bay.

That's it, You Guys! No exceptions!"

Nick is silent, looks at Jon, then the deck, thinking. . .

"Is that including a built-in Safety Margin?"

"It is, Nick.

It's Fifteen-Minutes and that's close to the bone. But you can't mess with that, understand me, CLEARLY! You too, Jon."

Nick takes the lead . . .

"We don't want to, ZAAN. . . Here's the
Plan, then. . . PREDITOR is going to
distract THE DCG ZEELAND to the far
Northern Perimeter of their Restriction
Zone.

Next, THE ROTTERDAM will come in and
Quick Launch the Beebe, while
maintaining Maritime Radio Silence the
first time, to the Drop Site. That way
if they signal you, you'll have an
excuse. Then, back off to the
coordinates right here, until it's time
to recapture the Beebe.

After you signal us, we'll do one last
distraction up North, then contact you
for the final pick-up."

"Damn, Nick, that's cutting it close
with that 'FAST' CG Cutter ZEELAND.
They've got a Twenty-Two Knot high
speed vessel there."

Nick continues without missing a beat.

"And when they contact you, if they do,
at that point your Maritime Radio will
be up - You'll then acknowledge
Commander VISSER, and get out quick. .
. Finally, we'll all Rendezvous at the
Newport Bay Dock and pick-up the wreck
salvage BULLION Samples for the
Certificate."

ZAAN reacts tongue-in-cheek, as he
looks at   Jon.

"So, Jon and Jennifer, huh?"

They ALL 'Laugh' and part company, as
Jon and Nick return to the PREDITOR to
prep Jennifer for the task ahead.

In moments, THE ROTTERDAM begins her
slower trek and alignment, Eight
Kilometers off the BLUE WALL at ST.
JORIS.

At the designated time, THE PREDITOR
comes alongside THE ROTTERDAM and drops
off the BEEBE Dive Team, as it then
makes FLANK Speed to the North End of
the RESTRICTION ZONE to distract the
DCG ZEELAND.

Chapter 21: THE ROTTERDAM'S ARRIVAL

THE ROTTERDAM REACHES THE BLUE WALL OFF
ST. JORIS BAY: Preparations are already
complete as Jon and Jennifer complete a
last systems check and the locks are
released to free the SPECIALIZED Mini-
Bathysphere from the Dive Bay.

At last, the BEEBE gradually moves into
the black water out of sight of the
ROTTERDAM's Moon Room Dive Bay heading
down the North facing of the BLUE WALL.

HUMMING of the Beebe's Twin Electric
Motors is the only SOUND breaking the
silence of the dive as Jon turns on the
Exterior Lights of the Beebe exposing
masses of various sized Fish and Coral
outcrops.

Then he powers up the Bathysphere to
Full Speed, quickly descending deeper
through the first thermocline. Gauges,
switches, lights, video monitors and
control panels light up the Beebe's
interior like a Christmas tree.

With COMMO headsets on, Jon maneuvers
the Dive Planes using only his
Joystick, as Jennifer smoothly
stretches over and kisses his cheek,
then grabs his crotch.

"Don't get too excited, that's just for Good Luck, Babe!"

"You can keep that up all night, Jen . . . Just don't take any of your clothes off!"

Jennifer laughs, then returns serious, to her seat on his right, doing her Final Check on the Manipulating Arms and all the safety gauges: including Oxygen, Nitrogen and various other interior Gas Levels.

Jennifer's about to finish the Check List, as they arrive at the third thermocline.

"Oxygen, Nitrogen and Gas Levels, Jen?"

"Check and Normal, and let's keep this formal, Babe, since this conversation is being recorded on my MARK! Now.

Safety Check List complete."

"Excellent, Jen. We've just passed the Third Thermocline.

Internal Pressure Status - Nominal at One Atmosphere - External Temperature - Three Degrees Celsius -

We are now descending through Six-Hundred Meters - Position is Seven Kilometers from our entry point."

"We should now be able to sight the wreckage of your submarine, Babe."

"U-boat, Jen. . . it's a U-boat. Let's keep it Official, as you said."

"Okay, Stuffy! U-boat. . ."

They BOTH begin intently viewing out their respective Portals.

BATHYSPHERE - NEAR SIX-HUNDRED METERS: A DISTANT VIEW of The Blue Wall at Six-hundred and Eighty Meters down - Lights pierce the black water, as abruptly, the U-Boat comes into view on a ledge just below them.

Jon and Jennifer stare out of the two pressure portals as . . .

"OH MY GAWD, Jon . . . It's there!"

"Incredible, Babe! Just incredible!"

Rocky outcrops along The BLUE WALL are lit up by the exterior lights of the Beebe as a few large Groupers and a Six Gill Shark swim nearby.

Jon carefully slows the Bathysphere's descent, as it hovers over the Three-Meter GASH in the aft HULL section of U-1055.

Jennifer moves both the robotic Arms into position.

"From now on, Jen, I'm video recording these events, since our Mothership ROTTERDAM is not directly connected to us by cable or transmission range.

I'm positioned Stationary above the opening of U-1055 and extending the Primary Camera Arm into the Aft Torpedo Room."

"Are you ready to move the Lift Arm into position, Jon?"

"Affirmative.

Give me control of the Lift Arm, Jen."

BATHYSPHERE CLOSE-UP VIEW: The Lift Arm begins moving into and through the opening.

Particulate is beginning to fill the Camera viewing area as the Arm movement stirs up silt from the Torpedo Room floor. Jon then moves the Lift to the broken Crate and grasps an Ingot.

A large Moray kicks up silt, as it moves out of the opening.

"I'm Moving the Lift Arm to recover an Ingot from that broken Crate.

What's it's weight, Jen?"

Jennifer Confirms back to him . . .

"Ten Kilograms or about 360 ounces.

Update, Captain Cutie . . .

Time On Site: Three Minutes -

Time Remaining: Seventeen Minutes"

Jennifer's laughing as. . .

"Hey, Hey. It's Captain Jon . . . Not Cutie.

Wow, that's heavy! And, it's worth almost 1.2 MILLION USD$, all by itself!"

The Arm moves the Ingot back to the hovering Beebe and places it into the 'Ballast Bay' on the underside of the hull.

The procedure is repeated several more times until the broken Crate is empty. When suddenly, a precipitous DEEP RUMBLE IS HEARD and Silt begins to completely block the camera view.

The U-Boat Hull VIBRATES and some small rocks unknown to Jon and Jennifer, fall off the ledge underneath the Hull, into the Abyss below.

"What was that, Jen?

Jennifer, STOP all operations, we might have destabilized the U-BOAT when we removed all that weight!"

"I don't know, Jon . . . It didn't sound good. . . Maybe we should get out of here.

Here's the Update . . .

Time On Site: Thirteen Minutes -

Time Remaining: Seven Minutes"

"If that happens again, Jen, we're through, understood."

"No problem. . . We can go now, if you want."

Some of the silt clears and the Camera Arm is repositioned over another Crate as the Lift Arm attempts to raise the Entire un-opened Crate.

Jon positions the Camera Arm and continues trying to move the robotic Lift Arm.

"What's it's weight, Jen?"

"One-Hundred and Four Point Eight Kilograms or about 3,650 ounces. That one crate is worth over $10.6 Million Dollars, Jon!"

"Can we lift that to the Beebe, Jen?

"The Arm is rated for ONLY Ninety-Five Kilograms. It will probably drop it, Jon."

"Let's try anyhow, since we've got a good grip on it. . . And we're almost out of time."

The Lift Arm clamps tighter on the short side of the Crate.

It begins to VIBRATE VIOLENTLY, as Jon struggles to lift the Gold Bullion Crate out of the opening. The Crate lifts it several more inches above the floor, then the Robotic ARM overloads. But, unfortunately, it locks up without releasing the Crate.

Precipitously, Silt explodes around the Camera and obscures everything.

"I think we're done here. . . Release that thing Jennifer! And check our Time, too!"

"Jon, it won't let go . . . It's become an anchor. . . It's holding us from moving, Jon. What have you done. . ."

"Stay cool, Babe. . . Again, what's our Time?"

"Time on Site: Eighteen Minutes -

Time Remaining: Two Minutes"

The silt clears enough for the Camera to be retracted.

INTERIOR VIEW OF THE BATHYSPHERE: Jon flips on the Red Zone Interior Lights of the Beebe exposing its mass of gauges and controls. Beside him, Jennifer is literally shaking with fear in her eyes, plus the cold on her skin, as he moves over and kisses her deeply.

"Hey Jen, since I'm the Captain of this damn ship, I'm now pronouncing us man and wife. And one of those Bullion Bars in our hold is your wedding ring!"

"Oh, GAWD, Jon . . . I Love you! But, please get us out of here, now!"

They can view the frozen arm from the Camera angle and the portals. Fear enters every nerve in both their bodies, as they fully realize they've anchored themselves to the U-Boat.

Unexpectedly, another slide of rocks and broken coral rumbles by them, as Jon tries to shake the Beebe loose from the Bullion Crate.

"Time, Jon! We've got to get out of here!"

"Okay, Babe, Okay! Just settle down. I need you to re-program the Camera arm. Bring the Camera to the storage bay and release it off the arm."

Jennifer quickly types commands and concentrates on her controls. She completes the tedious process in record time.

"What's our Time Update, Jen?"

"Time on Site: Twenty-One Minutes -

Time Remaining: Minus One Minute -

We only have a Ten-Minute reserve window, Jon. Now it's down to Nine."

"Listen to me, Jen. . . Mount the cutting torch onto your arm and manipulate it to my gripping arm. Then fire it up!"

EXTERIOR U-BOAT WRECK: Both Jon and Jennifer watch intently out her portal, directly into the gash in the U-boat's HULL. In moments, the blow-torch is mounted and is cutting a path through the main manipulating arm. . . As . . . BOOOOOM. . .

In an explosion of metal parts, the Main Arm breaks off from the Beebe and the Bullion crate literally disintegrates into the sand of the U-boat's Aft Torpedo room.

Gold Bullion Bars BLAST outward and scatter all over the floor. Several more Crates can be seen, but it's not clear how many remain in the empty Torpedo Room, as slit obscures their view.

"Retract and Store what's left of both arms in the Belly Cavity, Jen."

Through a portal, we see Jennifer as she finishes. Then begins sliding over to Jon, hugging him for all she's worth.

"Okay, Okay. . . Make Ready for Ascent.

And give me a Complete Systems Check, since we might have ruptured something, when we severed the Arm."

"Aye, Aye, Captain. . .

Oh, by the way. . .

I Do!"

Now, through a quickly fogging portal, we can see Jennifer planting a big kiss on Jon's lips, as she returns to her navigation control seat.

HUMMING SOUNDS of the Electric Motors fade away with the Beebe rising upward.

We're still focused on the U-Boat as we see, ascending away from the wreckage SITE eastward, back to the surface rendezvous location, the Beebe, as it begins to retrace its path back to the Mothership - ROTTERDAM

EXTERIOR U-BOAT - WIDE VIEW OF WRECK SITE: As the Beebe disappears out of view, some more rocks fall from under the U-Boat into the Abyss below.

And the same large Moray Eel from before, returns from the depths, re-entering his lair through the Hull opening in the Aft Torpedo Room; while in that same moment, all light defuses to darkness and fades into BLACK.

Chapter 22: THE SUBMERSIBLE OIL RIG

LAGOS OIL COMPANY'S SELF-PROPELLED OIL RIG: Several crewmembers are working various operational tasks on deck, as the giant Oil Rig moves silently through Two to Three-Foot swells at Seven-Knots, Southeastward off ST. JORIS BAY.

On the Upper Deck, Crewmen are preparing the Helicopter Pad for an arrival. In the far distance due South, planes can be seen landing at Willemstad's HATO AIRPORT on the Coast of Curacao.

INSIDE THE SUBMERSIBLE OIL RIG BRIDGE: High Tech Marine Control Systems, with a bank of Video Monitors, are being operated by several crewmembers as the RIG's Captain enters the Bridge. He grabs a microphone at his CONTROL DESK, then belts out a directive across the Bridge to the First Mate and the DECK Crew, in an obvious Texas drawl.

"Hold steady at Seven-Knots with a HEADING of South-Southeast.

And remember, 'YEWAL', we have a COMPANY Chopper with some Big 'DIC WAGS' and a Security Team on its way.

So stay sharp 'ON DECK' . . . And
'HERE' too. We don't want ANY
problems!"

HATO AIRPORT, CURACAO - PRIVATE HANGER:
Inside the HANGER Entrance, A Gulf
Stream VI Jet with unknown markings,
sits in the unlit rear section of the
Hanger. Two men with the latest UZI-PRO
weapons stand guard, as the Gulf
Stream's Pilots watch from a small
office nearby.

Dirk VAN DER ROO and several Israeli
Operatives, dressed in casual attire
are loading two rental cars and a van
with various equipment, weapons and
rucksacks.

At that moment, Dirk gets a cell call.
He switches from Hebrew to Dutch, as he
speaks.

"I've got to take this, Moshe!
Private."

His Israeli friend, NODS his approval.

Dirk then moves away from the group,
and speaks softly in English to the
caller.

PREDITOR - MAIN DECK: It's Petra on her
cell to him, with the latest update.

"Are they with you, Babe?"

HATO AIRPORT - PRIVATE HANGER: Dirk is still cautious as he speaks.

"Yeah, we're loading, but no defined Targets, yet. But how are You and Jennifer holding up . . . And how did the Beebe Dive go?"

PREDITOR — MAIN DECK: Petra continues in English. . .

"Jennifer and Jon are fine. They're here with me and Nick at Newport on the Yacht.

The TWO of them, plus ZAAN's crew found what you're looking for.

But the sample was limited to One-Hundred Kilos. And Nick is having trouble getting his friends in Amsterdam to issue the Salvage Certificate. . .

They appear to be as compromised, as the Assholes we have here in Curacao."

HATO AIRPORT - PRIVATE HANGER: Dirk is stoic, as he resumes.

"I expected that. We're simply going to have to take the High Road and assist the Israelis in recovering it."

PREDITOR — MAIN DECK: Petra reacts almost yelling into the cell phone. . .

"I can't believe you're saying that Dirk, after all we've been through."

HATO AIRPORT - PRIVATE HANGER: Dirk is resigned to reality . . .

"Calm yourself, Petra. After long discussions here with Moshe and OVERSEAS with TEL AVIV and my close friend BEN-ZION at MOSSAD, it's clear this IS, without a doubt, 'Holocaust Gold'.

'The Proof' is actually forged into each GOLD Ingot Bar. You can verify it for yourselves. If it's Not, we go it alone. You and Nick are not compromised, just me.

Just in case, I've got Pieter and Derrick nearby covering my back."

PREDITOR - MAIN DECK: Petra takes a deep breath. . .

"Okay, then, how do I need to verify them?"

HATO AIRPORT - PRIVATE HANGER: Dirk gets very serious now . . .

"First, let me just tell you this. . .

Ben-Zion confirmed to me that during the War, HEINRICH Himmler directed the Nazi SS to build an Ingot Forge under the HARZ Mountains in Central Germany.

They used forced Jewish labor from the nearby BUCHENWALD Concentration Camp.

When the workers were almost dead, they took them to NORDHAUSEN to die in the Ovens.

That Ingot Forge melted down Gold taken from Jews in the Camps from all over Germany, before and after they gassed them.

Gold jewelry, Coins, TEETH, Gold Bars, literally anything the Jews brought with them to the Camps."

PREDITOR — MAIN DECK: Petra's suddenly inflamed with hatred, as instantly she yell's out. . .

"GOD! It's ALL SO SICKENING!

AND NORDHAUSEN! That's where my Grandfather died, Dirk . . . His records even said he'd been working in an underground factory."

HATO AIRPORT - PRIVATE HANGER: Dirk shows no emotion as he adds . . .

"Well . . . For that, Babe, I'm truly SORRY! But it's the reality of this GOLD Bullion HOARD.

One Hundred tons was amassed until the end of the War in 1945.

They fully believe it's the same Gold, Himmler sent to Flensburg to load onto that U-Boat-1055.

And All those Gold Bars had the NAZI SWASTIKA and Six Numbers preceded by a Triangle-like emblem, forged into them.

The EMBLEM was the Hebrew letter SHIN 'W'.

So, judging from what you've told me, they're probably the same Bars in that U-Boat. And that Emblem will confirm it!"

Dirk goes SILENT, suddenly.

Precipitously, a young female Israeli Operative, SABRA, comes over to Dirk, as he stops talking. She smiles at him and speaks in Hebrew, obviously knowing he's talking to another woman.

"It's time, Dirk. The vehicles are loaded!"

PREDITOR — MAIN DECK: Petra hears the seductive voice of a woman talking. . .

"So, is that what you've been doing! While you've had me isolated out on this Yacht, baby-sitting your niece!"

HATO AIRPORT - PRIVATE HANGER: Dirk turns to acknowledge Sabra, as he smiles at her, then begins speaking in Dutch accented Hebrew.

"I'll be there in One, Sabra."

Dirk then returns to English to responds to Petra's inflamed voice. . .

"You know that's Not TRUE, Babe. This is Business.

But don't leave me, 'CAUSE, she'd make a fine substitute."

PREDITOR — MAIN DECK: Petra LAUGHS viciously. . .

"Yeah, and I'd have to Kill YOU BOTH!"

HATO AIRPORT - PRIVATE HANGER: Dirk laughs at her probably serious comment, then closes. . .

"I'll contact you in three hours, Petra."

Dirk then walks back to the Israeli Operatives - serious face . . . as He shuts Off the Cell and stores it in his Rucksack.

He then pulls out an IDF Digital Satellite COMMO Device and Logs In.

Chapter 23: THE SHIN REVELATION

ZAAN THIEL'S DIVE FACILITY - NEWPORT:
Jon, Jennifer and Nick's Crewmen are
completing the unloading of the Beebe
from the Moon Pool.

ZAAN and Nick enter the MOON POOL Dive
Bay. Nick has his Cell up to his ear.
It's Petra. No one but Nick hears her -
gushing, as Nick's face goes pale with
shock. . .

"Petra, You've Got to be kidding. I've
got over One-Hundred Thousand US$
invested in this thing. . ."

Nick gets even more nervous about
ZAAN's reaction, as he stresses out
from Petra's Revelation.

Nick tries to softens his voice. . .

"That MONEY won't go away. Who's going
to cover that!"

Abruptly, ZAAN turns and faces Nick.
He's overheard some of the conversation
and the word 'MONEY'. He knows, and
now, he too is incensed - something has
gone badly wrong.

"Damn, Nick! What's happening Now?"

Nick waves his arms to ZAAN, to calm him down, as he tries to listen, stunned at Petra's conversation. Petra gushes more, but still, no one but Nick can hear her.

Finally, Nick looks at ZAAN - speaking in Dutch.

"Petra's coming down here. . . Right now, ZAAN. She was just on a CALL to Dirk! She has some new Info for us."

Nick OFFS his phone, then searches for a distraction, as he looks to Jon and Jennifer.

"Jon, have you got our wreck spoils ready for viewing?"

Jon and a Crewman adjust the NOISY HYDRAULIC HOIST onto the Beebe and move the entire Beebe over a concrete pad beside the Moon-Pool Dive Opening. Jon goes to the Beebe with Jennifer and together they all begin unloading its External Storage Bay, "The Belly".

"Give us a minute, Nick!"

At Once, Jon, Jennifer and the Crewman all begin LAUGHING AND GRUNTING uncontrollably, while struggling to lift out the first Ten-Kilogram Gold Bars.

Everyone moves over to the Moon-Pool, to see why they're laughing as Jon remarks. . .

"Well, this should put a smile on someone's face today!"

ZAAN is staring intently at the softly gleaming object they're holding - his face transforms from a smile to a scowl.

ZAAN jocularly coughs out his first comment.

"Well, I must admit. . . I must look like a Dumb Ass Idiot. That's a Gold Bullion Bar!"

ZAAN gets LOUDER . . .

"That's Not Salvage. . . That's Treasure!"

Nick jumps in to calm ZAAN. . .

"Now wait a minute, ZAAN. Don't get your hackles up, just yet."

Jon begins LAUGHING again, as Jennifer takes out another GOLD Ingot by herself. . .

"I'd say your plan to disguise this as salvage to Mr. Thiel is wasted, Nick."

At that exact moment, Petra enters the Moon Pool Room from an Upper Deck. Catching everyone by surprise, she immediately rushes over to the GOLD Bullion Bar that Jennifer is now stacking in place.

CLOSE-UP: Petra seriously begins inspecting it, as everyone's attention is focused on her. Instantly, Petra's expression gets suddenly somber.

NOW FULLY Energized, she grabs the GOLD Bar and makes her announcement.

"This unfortunately, everyone. . . is, HOLOCAUST GOLD BULLION!"

She holds it up to Jon and Jennifer first, then walks over and hands it to Nick.

CLOSE-UP: Nick clearly sees the SHIN Emblem on the Bar — 'W' 179335 as he passes it to ZAAN for his inspection, then Petra continues.

"That Triangle-like Symbol in front of those Six Serial Numbers answers the long lost question.

It's the Voiceless HEBREW letter for SHIN, 'W'."

As she looks around, everyone's facial expression is in stunned MENTAL SHOCK.

"Unfortunately, this Gold belongs to Israel. And they, according to Dirk, are now in charge of its REPARIATION!"

Chapter 24: THE OIL RIG EVENT

THE LAGOS OIL SELF-PROPELLED DRILL RIG:
We can see a HELICOPTER Touchdown on
the UPPER DECK as Henrik VANBOVEEN and
his lead Security Team Officer Anders
arrive Late Morning in the first
Helicopter.

Landing with a contingent of Security
Operatives, immediately they're met by
the Rig's Captain and escorted to the
Bridge. A second Helicopter hovers
nearby arriving once the first one
leaves. Several additional Security
Operatives, including YANNA and Lugar,
are also met and escorted down into the
facility.

THE BRIDGE CON - LAGOS OIL RIG: Henrik
and Anders enter the Bridge and observe
operations as several Navigation
Crewmen work a battery of Video Screens
and High Tech Controls. The Rig's
Captain adds his comments, by first
pointing to several Control Joysticks
at his CONSOLE.

"Gentlemen, what you see here is not
unlike a NASA Shuttle - flying in
Space. We have Yaw, Pitch, Roll,
Vertical Height, Horizontal . . ."

Immediately, Hendrik interrupts him. Then redirects the conversation to his prime objective.

"Enough, Captain. We need only two objectives here. How quickly you can get us to our Target Coordinates and set up Dive operations.

And how we can go about removing our Assets from that Massive Depth and get them up here On Deck for TRANSPORT."

Obviously, any further discussion is needless as the Captain MOTIONS for a Supervisor. But he still reacts undeterred.

"Well Sir, we'll be over that Target in less than thirty minutes. Then, we'll flood the Rig's Pontoons, adjust pressures and be ready for Dive Operations by 1300 Hours.

Our Divers have been ready all morning."

The Captain pauses and looks over at another Man as he continues. . .

"Now on that other question, I've got Mr. Johnson here from Houston Texas to help out. He's a Master TOOLPUSHER and my Chief Supervisor.

A big man, typical tough Oil Rig type, six foot five walks over and eyeballs Henrik.

He as well, speaks, with a heavy Texas drawl.

"Fortunately, the information your people got me early this morning gave me enough to complete my modifications. The Deep Divers will have a modified MUD Return Pipe at the Target Site to pull up your Heavy Salvage."

He then scans around the Bridge staring at the enormous Armed Security Contingent seeming to GUARD Hendrik.

"Your Forty-Pound Weight Maximums will be equal to typical SHALE ROCK that we separate from MUD here On Deck at our SHALE SHAKER. You'll simply go to the SHAKER and retrieve your Salvage. . . That's about it."

VANBOVEEN 'waves' his Security Team over!

"Okay then, let's meet with the Divers, Captain."

All Visitors and the Captain leave the Bridge into a blinding bright sunlight to go down to the Diver Operations Room.

As the afternoon progresses, the SUBMERSIBLE OIL RIG gets positioned over THE BLUE WALL.

Dive Operations begin without delay. Initially, the work is tedious as each DIVE team gets acclimated, but soon the GOLD Bullion Bars begin to arrive up the pipes from the U-Boat and slowly fill the Shaker Grid.

THE PONTOON AREA OF THE SELF-PROPELLED RIG: By the time it turns Dusk, the Crews are taking a well-deserved, Three-hour break for Dinner and Rest as a Dark Overcast Moonless sky covers the operation Zone.

HEAVY WAVES AND WIND BATTER the Pontoons and Ballast Tanks at the Ocean surface of the Oil Rig. While stabilizers and electric drive motors are GRINDING AWAY LOUDLY working overtime, to keep the RIG immobile against the elements.

By Midnight, the SOUNDS have become routine and monotonous, as the situation is about to change. . .

In the shadowy areas at the Ocean's surface around the Pontoons, silently and without warning, what appears to be Navy Seals in black wet-suits appear, then surface at all four Pontoons of the Oil Rig.

Dirk, Pieter and Derrick use night diving suits, re-breathers and night-vision goggles to gain stealthy access to the Northwest Pontoons of the Oil Rig Platform.

Using specialized rope apparatus, they climb up fifteen meters to the primary Underdeck Structure and secure their gear.

At the same time, Moshe, Sabra and two seasoned KIDON OPERATIVES, DOV and RAVIV gain access to the Southeast Pontoons and perform the same operation.

Above and oblivious to all of this, because of NOISE from the DEEP WATER PUMP and the BULLION recovery operation drowning out any other sounds, Security Guards with automatic weapons casually patrol the upper Decks.

Spot Lights and Flood Lights on the Upper Rig Decks are blazing everywhere, as Operations continue.

As the PUMP and recovery operation continues, several Security Operatives are removing, cleaning and stacking Gold Bullion Bars 'spit-out' of the pipes, like the SOUND OF SLEDGE HAMMERS POUNDING STEEL RAIL SPIKES.

The Bullion Bars are continually filling the Shaker grid along with sea water, silt and slurry sucked up from the U-Boat below, as it slushes over the side of the RIG.

Moshe gives the Ready Signal and Dirk responds, as tiny remote sighting cameras pop-up and view the situation on the Main Upper Deck.

Suddenly, grappling and rappelling ropes are launched.

Everything starts happening at once.

PHFT! -PHFT! -PHFT! -PHFT! - Uzi-Pros with sound suppressors take out the Security Guards at each perimeter.

Dirk and Moshe's teams take cover and re-group on each side of the Deck.

Dirk moves to the nearest Armed Security Operative at the Shaker. Drawing his weapon, the Operative fires blind - RATTATTATTAT!

RATTAT! He's strafing the Deck wildly, as Dirk reaches him - a crushing arm around his throat. He tries to fire again. Too late. Dirk cracks his neck in one movement, as his machine pistol strafes LOUDLY a final time, RATTATTATTAT!

Dirk turns to the next man. Another Security Operative, ready with his Long Knife drawn. Wrong Weapon. Dirk adjusts and reverses his thrust in one movement. The Knife impaling into the man's gut as he tries to break away.

Moving wildly to escape - Dirk pulls him back, arm around his neck, again a crushing windpipe move. The man falls limp.

Dirk moves toward the nearby Hatch. From below, two more Guards arrive at the ready onto the Main Deck. Dirk has the first one, but the second man takes deadly aim at Dirk.

Suddenly three silenced rounds blow away the second Guard's upper chest as Sabra moves out of the shadows LAUGHING, then smiles at Dirk, just as he throws the first Guard's body over the railing into the Sea. He's grinning back at her as she comments in Hebrew.

"Good work, for and Old Man."

Dirk LAUGHS. His grin gets even bigger, as he adds in Hebrew.

"You wouldn't rate me so low, if you were in my Bed, Little Girl!"

PHFT! -PHFT! -PHFT! -PHFT! -PHFT! -PHFT!

At once, silenced rounds fly in against the deck around them, from the Upper HELO Pad.

Both of them roll in opposite directions sideways. Sabra targets the shooter first. Her round hits his neck, as he falls into the sea clutching his throat, GURGLING LOUDLY.

More rounds unsilenced, RATTATTATTAT, tear across the Deck.

Dirk's round hits the shooter's chest, blowing him backward, but Sabra hits that MARK too at the same moment, knocking him off the HELO Pad. Suddenly nothing's moving.

They can only hear the LOUD PULSING NOISE of the Mud Pump and Bullion Bars ejecting GOLD BARS, LIKE HAMMERS onto the Shaker Screen.

Instinctively, they both turn ready to fire, as the watertight Hatch OPENS again.

Moshe, DOV, and Pieter emerge sporting about twenty-five captors from the Bridge and Crew Quarters, hands bound in nylon military hand-ropes. Dirk speaks first in Dutch.

"Where's Derrick, Pieter?"

"RAVIV has him, down below. He took a-round in the side, but he's good."

Without warning, a CHOPPER SOUND ERUPTS from the HELO Pad.

The Helicopter lifts away gaining traction over the SOUNDS of the Shaker.

VANBOVEEN looks down at them from the Copilot position, as the HELO quickly moves away to the Northwest.

Moshe and Dirk, just watch it disappear into the night sky, as Moshe chortles.

"We'll find him, my friend."

Dirk winks at Sabra. . .

"I have, No Doubt, about that Moshe, No Doubt."

Chapter 25: THE FINAL RECKONING

HAIFA BAY- ISRAEL - THREE WEEKS LATER:
WE ENJOY LONG VIEWS, TO THE DISTANT SEA
. . . It's gorgeous Mediterranean
Weather with Bright Sunlight filling
every shadow. Strong Twenty-Five Knot
NOISY COASTAL BREEZES, WHOOSHING Kite-
surfers and Windsurfers up and down the
Beach Zone South of the City of Haifa.

Northeast of there, in the center of
the expansive blue waters of Haifa Bay,
Nick's Yacht — PREDITOR - drifts at
anchor.

The Yacht is waiting for a Naval
Destroyer to arrive with a very
important Dignitary.

At the same time, two High Tech Israeli
Naval Cutters are at 'All Stop' about a
Thousand-Meters to their stern, at the
Entrance to Haifa Bay.

THE YACHT'S REAR DINNER DECK: Dirk,
Nick and Moshe are sitting at an
outside Banqueting Table above the
Launch Deck, smoking cigars and
LAUGHING.

At the Stern and below them, Jon and Jennifer are preparing to Lift-off from the Launch Deck and Kitesurf. . .

At least, until the Dignitary's Boarding Party arrives at the Yacht.

Both embrace and kiss each other, as Jennifer points to, then waves, her new engagement ring at her Uncle.

Dirk LAUGHING - relights his cigar, then gives her his thumbs up signal, while Jon and Jennifer launch their Kites into the wind and lift-off into Haifa Bay.

"Did you see the look on that Swiss Banker's face yesterday, when we had him come down to the Dive Room to inventory all those Nazi Gold Bullion Ingots."

Moshe puffs on his cigar, smiling. . .

"It was a thrill for me, Dirk. Over Ten-Billion in Gold Bullion BARS. You know, he wasn't Jewish. His family actually ran our Bank in Zurich when the Nazi's threatened us in 1939. His father along with the Swiss Defense Forces in Zurich ousted the Nazi SS Officers, when they came to raid our Bank, and several other Jewish controlled Banks in Switzerland.

The Nazi's never came back."

Dirk changes the subject as he sees Moshe getting teary eyed.

"Well, I'm glad we've finally turned that Hoard of Bounty over to YOUR Security Forces, now. It's where it should be!"

Nick belts down another Polar, as he LAUGHS BANTERINGLY.

"Yeah, that's a relief, . . . Duh! Tossing Out Ten-Billion Big Ones, without so much as a juicy Kiss to show for it, Ha - No Shit!"

Dirk shakes his cigar at Nick, then switches to Dutch.

"Okay, Okay, Nick! Don't be such a BAD SPORT! I've got your point. . .

Directly between my eyes. . . You Ole Salt."

OVERHEAD POV: Suddenly, Jon flies in over the top of all of them, as his Kite pulls him even higher. He then turns for the water and kicks up a Three-Meter Rooster Tail, as he rushes off toward the Israeli Naval Cutters.

Dirk takes another puff off his Cigar and turns back to face Moshe - more matter of fact.

"When did they tell you they'd be here, Moshe?"

Moshe looks at his watch.

"He was just leaving the Knesset, when I spoke to him, last. I'd say they'll be here by Two -- 1400 Hours."

Moshe watches Jon and Jennifer as they do some more air flips and helicopters around the Yacht.

"Those Kids are incredible, Dirk. . .

You know we have an Israeli Kitesurfing Team that would love to meet them. Maybe you could stay over for a few days, and I'll make the arrangements."

Dirk slowly takes another long drag off his cigar.

"I think they would Love that, Moshe. And I personally, would enjoy a few days of R&R around here, too."

Dirk grins at Nick and LAUGHS.

"What do You think about that, Nick?"

Nick finishes his Polar, then turns observing the Yachts sexy new Hire! A Russian Concierge named YANNA, standing behind him, as he begins chuckling at Dirk. . .

"As long as you're paying, Dirk.

Hey, YANNA. Get me another Polar, Honey!"

YANNA winks at Nick, as she moves quickly off to the Galley.

Out of the blue, Moshe CLEARS HIS THROAT for attention - then interrupts Nick, with a wave of his cigar.

He's grinning mischievously at both Dirk and Nick. . .

"Actually, we're paying Nick! I was saving this until the Prime Minister arrived, but He's Late. So, I might as well tell you both, without DELAY!"

Moshe, takes another drag off his cigar.

"Two things actually. The Knesset voted unanimously this morning, to make the first Holocaust Gold Repatriation payment of One-Million US$ Dollars, to Curacao's Mikvé Synagogue.

You should BOTH know, it's the oldest active Jewish congregation in the New World.

Besides, as we all know, Curacao is where the Gold BULLION was actually recovered in the first place.

Nonetheless, and this is the best part! They also voted unanimously to give You and Dirk and Your Team, a One-Percent Finders-Fee for helping us Discover U-1055. . . And of course, Recover the GOLD Bullion."

YANNA returns, smiling at Nick, handing him his fresh ice-cold Polar. She then, steps back out of sight, but Not out of listening range.

Dirk's eyes bulge, as he coughs-out smoke from his cigar, he's really energized - then laughs back at Nick, and yells.

"GOOD GAUD, Nick! That's Over, $100 Million Dollars, at today's Bullion prices!"

Without thinking, Nick jumps up and hugs Dirk, as Jon and Jennifer sail by, and see them all going nuts down below.

Together, Dirk and Nick YELL OUT to Jon and Jennifer flying above the open Bay.

"Oooh 'Raah!"

Then, Nick yells back to YANNA. . .

"YANNA! Break Out that DOM PERIGNON & VEUVE CLICQUOT. . .

Tonight, it's 'Par'tayh' Time on PREDITOR!"

THE END